HERITAGE CHURCHES

of the Indigenous Peoples of British Columbia

Historical Events & Architectural

Elements of Church Structures

Kenneth E. Perry

ISBN-13: 978-0-88839-074-5   [trade edition paperback]
ISBN-13: 978-0-88839-304-3   [epub version]

Library and Archives Canada Cataloguing in Publication

Title: Heritage churches of Indigenous Peoples of British Columbia : historical events &
    architectural elements of church structures / Kenneth E. Perry.
Names: Perry, K. E. (Kenneth Edwin), 1943- author.
Identifiers: Canadiana 20190123257 | ISBN 9780888390745 (softcover)
Subjects: LCSH: Church buildings—British Columbia—History. | LCSH: Church architecture—British
    Columbia—History. | LCSH: Church buildings—British Columbia—History—Pictorial works. | LCSH:
    Church architecture—British Columbia—History—Pictorial works. | LCSH: Indians of North America—
    British Columbia—Religion. | LCSH: British Columbia—History, Local. | LCSH: British Columbia—
    Church history.
Classification: LCC NA5246.B7 P47 2019 | DDC 726.509711—dc23

Printed in China

PRODUCTION & DESIGN: M. Lamont & L. Raingam
EDITOR: D. MARTENS

We acknowledge the financial support of the Government of Canada through the Canada Book Fund and the Canada
Council for the Arts, and of the Province of British Columbia through the British Columbia Arts Council and the Book
Publishing Tax Credit.

*Hancock House gratefully acknowledges the Semiahmoo, Kwantlen, Katzie and Lummi First
Nations, whose unceded traditional territories our offices reside upon.*

hancock

house

Published simultaneously in Canada and the United States by
HANCOCK HOUSE PUBLISHERS LTD.
19313 Zero Avenue, Surrey, B.C. Canada V3Z 9R9
(604) 538-1114   Fax (604) 538-2262
HANCOCK HOUSE PUBLISHERS
#104-4550 Birch Bay-Lynden Rd, Blaine, WA, U.S.A. 98230-9436
(800) 938-1114   Fax (800) 983-2262
www.hancockhouse.com   sales@hancockhouse.com

British Columbia - Regional Map

FORT NELSON

KITWANGA

FORT ST. JAMES CHETWYND

PRINCE
GEORGE

QUESNEL

WILLIAMS
LAKE

CAMPBELL
RIVER

POWELL
RIVER

CACHE
CREEK

KAMLOOPS

MERRITT KELOWNA

INVERMERE

VANCOUVER

PENTICTON

VICTORIA

CRANBROOK

LEGEND

REGION ONE - Vancouver Island & Gulf Islands

REGION TWO - Lower Mainland & Coast Mountain:

REGION THREE - Thompson Okanagan

REGION FOUR - Kootenay Rocky Mountain

REGION FIVE - Cariboo Chilcotin West

REGION SIX - Northern

TABLE OF CONTENTS

REGION - THREE : Thompson Okanagan

REGION – FOUR : Kootenay and Rocky Mountains

FOREWORD

Since first contact, church architecture in British Columbia has taken on many forms, some with extremely elaborate designs and others more modest. Each in its own way took on the daunting task of establishing an overall sense of reverence and honor, not only in the exterior of the structure but within as well. These were places of sacred worship.

The earliest churches began as rudimentary log structures, later on covered in horizontal or vertical clapboard siding, with moldings and elegant windows.

This book specifically looks at First Nations church structures through photographs of buildings that existed at the time of writing throughout British Columbia. It aims to demonstrate the architectural beauty of the numerous designs used in church buildings, whether plainly built or beautifully adorned with intricately designed stained-glass windows, fancy belfries, steeples, crockets, finials and roofs featuring overlapping rows of cedar shingles, all of which add to the buildings' character.

In early times on the frontier churches developed an interesting architecture in various styles, shapes, and sizes that evolved slowly over time. Notably influential were architects of churches of the Roman Catholic, Salvation Army, Pentecostal, Anglican, United, Full Gospel, Indigenous Shaker and Methodist denominations.

Over time, a large number of old churches have succumbed to the elements or to fire or abandonment, a sad trend that continues to this day. Some traditional churches have been replaced by modern buildings and some by new log structures, a practice that has brought old building traditions full circle.

Most of these churches, with the exception of the abandoned ones, are still used by First Nations believers on a regular basis, while some are opened only on special occasions such as weddings, funerals and community events. The survival of these structures has largely depended on the continued efforts of First Nations people.

During the 1800s, Christian influence was brought to bear on First Nations people throughout all regions of the province. The transition from aboriginal spirituality to Christianity as understood by missionaries of European settler background was more complicated than it has sometimes been depicted.

It would be a great injustice to the First Nations people to reduce their spiritual beliefs to a simplistic set of rules, stories or principles. In fact, aboriginal spirituality is a deeply sacred and complex system that evolved over thousands of years and, despite determined efforts by the colonial powers to stamp it out, has persisted and is deeply entwined with indigenous identity.

Notwithstanding the differences in spiritual practice throughout the various regions of British Columbia, the nomadic lifestyle of most indigenous people established a degree of cultural exchange through trading and other activities, and in turn fostered an intercultural set of spiritual concepts among the native communities.

Giving thanks for all things that gave life, direction and meaning was a daily practice. Whatever played a role in the cycle of life—Mother Earth, plants, animals, trees, wind, sun, the Creator and much more—were key elements in the indigenous spiritual tradition.

The adaptation between traditional beliefs and Christianity was seemingly a relatively tolerant process from the indigenous perspective, and as a result Christian churches quickly became permanent structures within most aboriginal villages. Many of the early churches still stand as a reminder of early Christian influence.

Architecturally, First Nations churches are magnificent works of art, often combining the designs of the clergy, professional architects and indigenous craftsmen alike. In many instances, they were constructed primarily by aboriginal workers.

The 2016 Canadian Census indicates there were 125,635 indigenous people in British Columbia, of which two-thirds identified as Christian, even in the wake of findings of the 2008–2015 Truth and Reconciliation Commission on Residential Schools; these Christian believers continue to grow in numbers.

Throughout the many years of research for this book, Ken was always greeted most graciously by the First Nations people. He had many remarkable conversations relating to these old and unique church buildings, historically and architecturally.

He was also invited to take photographs and to tour these outstanding structures for the purpose of a published work.

ACKNOWLEDGEMENTS

It is indeed a great pleasure to acknowledge the overwhelming support of my wife, Carol, my son, Ken, and my good friends Helga Pennel, Maureen Delorme, and Morrice Gauthier, all of whom were with me at one time or another, seeking out First Nations churches throughout British Columbia.

I also extend my sincere appreciation and gratitude to Margo Elewonibi for her help in providing valuable information on British Columbia First Nations.

TERMINOLOGY

For the purpose of this work the term Indigenous Peoples of British Columbia is now more commonly used. Other terms such as Native, Indian, Aboriginal or First Nations peoples may also be referenced.

While these terms are still being used to describe First Inhabitants of Canada they have also evolved to the now preferred term as Indigenous People.

PREFACE

During my research for a previous book called Frontier Forts and Posts of the Hudson's Bay Company, I could not help but notice that there were many First Nations communities in close proximity to these sites. I also noticed that many of these communities had churches, most of which were very old and unique, architecturally speaking. It was at this point that I started venturing out to various communities, compiling historical information and photographing these fascinating structures.

Many of these distinctive, handcrafted wooden structures have succumbed to the harsh elements of nature, fire and occasional abandonment. These great buildings are disappearing at a troubling rate, a trend that will probably continue for some time to come.

The architectural designs and workmanship of the buildings that no longer stand represented a legacy of aboriginal carpentry skills and great effort that should never be forgotten.

While some of these designs and skills can still be seen in existing structures throughout the country as witness of times past, the loss of others underscores the need to record existing structures for the generations that follow.

History not recorded cannot be reflected upon. The present, of course, is the time to engage in safekeeping and restoration—a gift to all those yet to come.

The photographs contained in this book represent the majority, though not all, of the churches that remain.

Architecture has always interested me, especially that of old wooden structures that are often left to wither away and be forgotten forever. Each of these old churches has a story to tell and a legacy to reveal. In this case, the story is about local history, while brief in content, and the legacy is about preserving through photographs the architectural elements of these irreplaceable church structures. I trust that I have accomplished this goal and brought to life the uniqueness of these many intriguing and sacred places of worship.

PUBLISHERS NOTE

During this important era of truth & reconciliation, we believe it is important to first acknowledge the atrocities that Indigenous Peoples faced from provincial, territorial and federal governments since colonization in Canada began. In addition, recognizing the persecution, destruction and loss of many cultural elements of First Nations peoples as a result of religious and government organisations actions may have had positive intentions, but ultimately has led to the loss of much cultural diversity across this vast country.

Over 150,000 First Nations children attended some 132 residential schools established across Canada by the Canadian government and with the help of the Catholic, United, Anglican and Presbyterian churches between 1857 and 1996. While intentions of these groups at the time may have been honourable, and likely in some cases, less so, the ultimate result was a severe loss and extinction of some Indigenous cultural elements, including language, art and other cultural expressions- including First Nations religious practices.

As a publishing house with a long history of producing works with Indigenous content, particularly focusing on the Pacific Northwest region, we were initially hesitant of pursuing this title given the justifiable scrutiny that religious organisations have faced in regards to their historic treatment of First Nations Peoples and the role that churches played during this time.

After some careful consideration, we believed the author demonstrated a true desire to showcase some of the unique architectural and historic elements of many of these old structures that were slowly returning back to the earth from which they were originally derived. Given no other publication that we could find had made such a strong attempt to capture these old buildings in written or photographic form, we believed this represented an opportunity to ensure that whatever unique Indigenous elements that had been incorporated into these buildings was not lost as well.

We hope the reader, particularly the Indigenous ones, might be able to glean some sense of appreciation and interest in the convergence of the colonial and Aboriginal cultures and how these were expressed at a local level at each one of these churches. These historic buildings may also act as a reminder of how societal and cultural believe and perspectives have changed over time.

-- HANCOCK HOUSE PUBLISHERS

Dedicated to all First Nations people in British Columbia.

May their struggles for equality and prosperity
bring good fortune and great happiness.

Eagles and Eagle Feathers
Spiritual Symbols of the First Nations people

The Eagle is one of many spiritual symbols of the First Nations People throughout British Columbia. This majestic bird represents wisdom, great strength, courage, power and protection.

Eagles are believed to have a special connection to the Creator, a connection that exists above and apart from the material world. The eagle is considered to be a messenger of the people and is given the privilege of conveying their prayers between the material world and the spirit world, where the Creator and past generations dwell.

REGION - ONE

VANCOUVER ISLAND & GULF ISLANDS

ST. ANN'S - OLD STONE - BUTTER CHURCH - 1870

Comiaken Hill – Cowichan Valley

In 1858 Father Pierre Rondesault arrived in Victoria and a year later set out to establish a mission in the Cowichan Valley. After his arrival in the area he built a church, it was a small modest log structure, he also built a cabin sparsely outfitted with a bed and a few other meager furnishings like a table and a single chair.

By 1870 Father Rondesault set out once again to build another church, this time much larger and more robust in structure; a church that could last a life time. With the help of the Cowichans, Father Rondesault began the arduous task of building a solid stone church high up on a barren piece of land called Comiaken Hill, which over looks Cowichan Bay. He funded the construction work with the proceeds from the sales of butter provided by the mission dairy farm.

At the behest of the Bishop of the Diocese, the stone church was to be abandoned essentially leaving it to the mercy of the elements of nature and vandalism. Father Rondesault moved on, and began the construction of a third church in 1880, a short distance down the road; it would be named St. Ann's. The site of this church was, in the opinion of the Bishop a more desirable location.

The old stone church now almost 140 years old has weathered the years, while somewhat overtaken by local plant life,

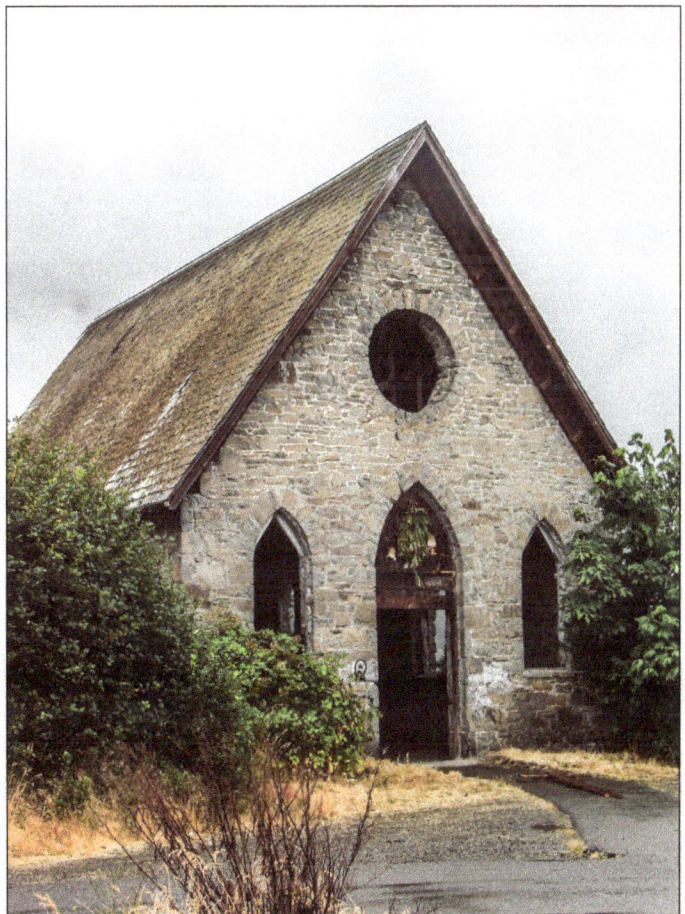

this church embodies the original architectural elements and designs of a past long ago. Built of stone that was quarried near by and intricately cemented together to form a Gothic style church of a kind found in many areas of Quebec.

The pointed arched window openings, door entranceway and circular feature window design certainly brings out an element of stone masonry of ancient times. Incorporated at each corner of the building are large stone buttresses giving it substantial strength and support to the side walls.

The beautiful stained glass windows and main doors which are no longer evident there, can be seen at St. Paul's Church on Salt Spring Island. On the peak of the roof near the front gable end was at one time an impressive six posted bell tower that supported a dome top and a large cross, essentially expressing a dramatic and remarkable appearance to the façade.

The exterior of course leaves little to comment on except to bring attention to the elaborately exposed scissor-trusses that highlights the internal roof structure; it is clear that at one time the ceiling was enclosed. In addition there are several hand crafted arched timbers that formed the sanctuary, a place where the alter would have been located. Somewhere along the way, several iron tie bars were installed to maintain the structural integrity of the roofs skeletal structure.

Restoration attempts to the old Butter Church were made in 1922 and again two more times in subsequent years, a revival process that fell short of achieving the ideals and aspirations of a man from St. Norbert, Quebec by the name of Father Pierre Rondeault. Father Rondeault died on April 11, 1900 at St. Joseph Hospital in Victoria.

St. Ann's, July 2009.

St. Ann's, c. 1910.
Photo courtesy of Royal BC Museum Archives

Along Cowichan Bay - A Ruined Chapel, Vancouver Island, B.C.

St. Ann's, c. 1900.
Photo courtesy of
Royal BC Museum
Archives

ST. ANN'S CHURCH
- 1903

- Cowichan -

After abandoning the Old Stone–Butter Church in 1880, Father Rondesault began building St. Ann's First Nation Parish Church a mile or so down the road.

In 1902, the new church burned to the ground. However, it was quickly rebuilt in 1903. Father Rondesault, who died in Victoria on April 11, 1900, never saw the second church by the same name, which still stands today. He was laid to rest under a red brick chapel at the rear of the church, where he is remembered.

St. Ann's Church stands majestically, high on a hillside overlooking the picturesque valley of the Cowichan. It is a very large church, with an equally large, imposing bell tower with an integrated front entrance.

The main windows are in the typical gothic style on both sides and on the façade as well. Over the front windows are two large, five-spoke wheel windows. A tall, four-sided bell-cast style steeple completes the tower.

The two front doors are solidly built and incorporate many handcrafted scenes done in the aboriginal tradition; a simple, arched frame unites the entrance doors and a three-panel window.

CHRIST CHURCH
- 1892

– Cormorant Island – Alert Bay

Cormorant Island lies off the northeast coast of Vancouver Island, near the forestry-based town of Port McNeill.

The small island was apparently named after a British ship that operated in the area in the mid-1800s. On the south side of the island is a fairly sheltered anchorage called Alert Bay, also evidently named after a ship that visited the area.

An Anglican Church was established at Alert Bay—prefabricated in England in 1879, so the story goes—and erected in 1892 under the supervision of the local priest. A sign in front of this church indicates the parish was founded in 1879, thirteen years prior to the assembly of this building.

This outstanding 1892 wooden church is a unique work of art unparalleled anywhere in British Columbia. Special architectural details abound, including exceptional elaborate trim work along the eaves, gables and bell tower. The detail around windows, doors and corners resembles the stone construction methods of the English tradition.

Along the rooftop, bell tower and covered porch, it reveals a fine example of cresting that is rarely seen today in wooden church construction. Particular attention was given to the bell tower, perhaps a one-of-a-kind structure. It is overwhelmingly embellished with myriad impressive architectural elements.

Adjacent to Christ Church is St. George's Chapel, established in 1925. It is, of course, small, but is a charming structure in its own right. While unadorned for the most part, it does have a couple of endearing features, such as the three decorative split-pane windows on the side

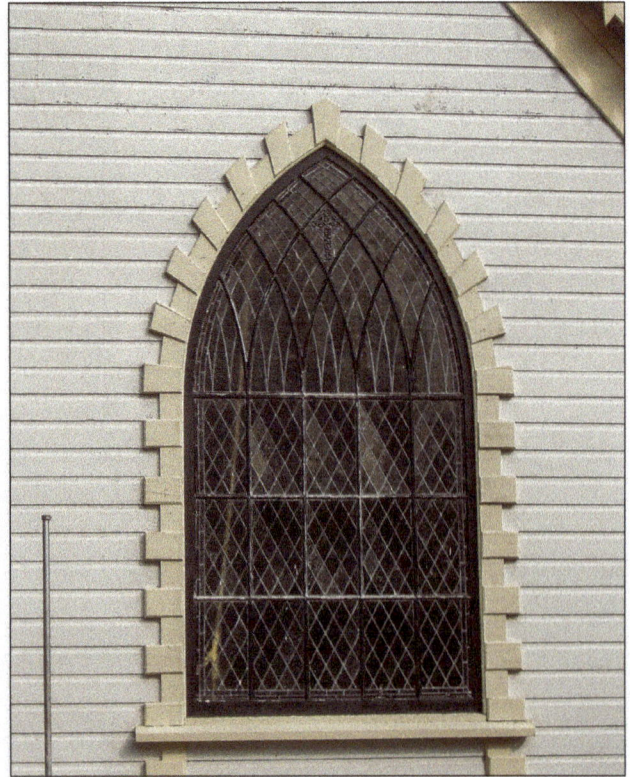

of the chapel, each pane artfully sectioned, complete with one oval-shaped crest-like pattern depicting a fleur-de-lis. Flanking the double front doors are smaller single-pane windows with the same designs.

QUADRA ISLAND UNITED CHURCH
- 1931

– Cape Mudge –

During Captain George Vancouver's circumnavigation in 1792 around what was subsequently named Vancouver Island, he came across a smaller island a short distance off the shore of a place now called Campbell River; he named it Quadra Island, to commemorate his conference with Commander Juan Francisco de la Bodega y Quadra at Nootka Sound.

Quadra Island is the largest of 11 islands in the Discovery Islands group and has a population of about 2,700. Besides the many industrial and sporting activities on and around the island, it offers a pleasant rural lifestyle and a refreshing atmosphere.

At the southern end of the island, at a place called Cape Mudge, stands a classic 1931 British Columbia heritage church by the name of Quadra Island United Church. This church, with its offset corner tower, incorporates two distinct sections, topped with a spire.

The bottom section combines two awesome cedar doors, embellished with two carved vertical elements flanking a large pair of ornate wrought-iron door handles. The carving is done in a native motif suggestive of the skills of a local artisan. Above the doors is a small spoke-wheel window.

The upper section, which contains the church bell, is a little more elaborate than the bottom section; it is plainly shingled on all sides. At the top edge of the tower are three flat, triangular-pointed elements placed between similarly designed pinnacles that are located at each corner. A short, unassuming spire with a four-section diamond-shaped finial completes the tower structure.

A striking arched stained-glass window accents the façade and is extremely detailed, in many colours. The scene depicts a fishing boat, waves, wind, land and the sun. It's an excellent composition representing the local industry.

On the side of the church proper as well as on the smaller addition to the rear are five windows, all adorned with lace-like mullions separating window panes around the perimeter—a very delicate detail that brings a certain quality and elegance to the overall design.

HOUSE OF PRAYER

Alert Bay – Cormorant Island

Just off the northwest coast of Vancouver Island lies a small kidney-shaped island with most of the amenities a small community requires. This island, called Alert Bay, is the homeland of the Namgis First Nation. It is also the site of the world's tallest totem pole and home of the orca, also known as the killer whale, a place of harmony and a peaceful atmosphere.

A short distance from Christ Church is an unassuming Pentecostal church called House of Prayer. It is a conventional house, cheerful and plainly built.

The inside is relatively sparse compared to traditional churches. However, this remains a place where like-minded people gather to worship. The lectern, while plain, is nicely adorned with an intricately carved arch over a pair of hands in prayer.

On the wall directly behind the lectern is a wall tapestry of sorts bearing the words of the Lord's Prayer. On the left side are various pieces of audio equipment used for praise and worship.

The House of Prayer is a modest little church that evokes an unquestionable feeling of being in a welcoming place.

ST. MICHAEL'S CHURCH
- 1892

– Cortes Island –

Cortes Island, population 945, is a small, quiet community and one of the most picturesque of the thousands of islands along the coast of British Columbia. The island is situated off Desolation Sound to the east and on the northern end of the Strait of Georgia. On a clear day, the area offers spectacular views in all directions.

Cortes Island was named after the Spanish conqueror of Mexico, Hernando Cortes, and was apparently given this name by Cayetano Valdez, a Spanish navy commander and mapmaker who explored the coastal waterways in 1793.

On the west side of the island, at a place called Squirrel Cove, there is a charming old church by the name of St. Michael's. This delightful little church takes a dominant position in the middle of a small First Nation community whose people have lived in the region for many centuries. They are very friendly and welcoming.

This church is a typical rectangular, one-level structure; the façade is completed by a two-step bell tower. The octagonal drum has pointed, arched, louvered vents topped off by an eight-sided shingled roof. The windows are of the gothic style, except the circular stained-glass window that depicts an eagle perched on top of a cross. This is an absolutely stellar rendering of native art and a beautiful way to express the spiritual ways of the people.

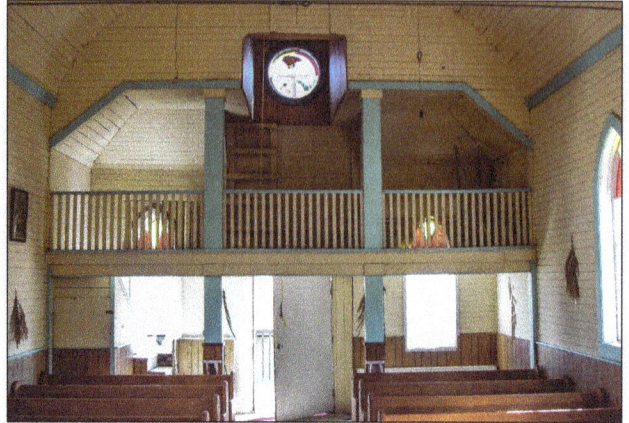

Upon entering the front door, the first impressions are of peace and harmony. The central focal point is a plainly constructed altar comprising three distinct panels, each decoratively carved with diamond-shaped elements.

The pews are rather appealing and solidly built but appear to be a relatively new addition to the church, perhaps no more than a decade old. The arched sections of the windows are highlighted by red and yellow stained-glass segments, while the lower area of the windows has clear square glass panes, essentially combining upper and lower elements in a modest composition.

Modern paneling surrounds the lower perimeter of the walls to imitate wainscoting. Over the front door area is a balcony with a rather plainly built balustrade.

The interior and exterior appearance of this fine church is quite attractive and well maintained, considering the climate of the region.

INDIGENOUS SHAKER CHURCH

- Brentwood Bay –

Just a short distance north of the thriving capital city of Victoria is the Saanich Peninsula, where farming and urban lifestyles peacefully coexist in a stretch of picturesque countryside.

At Fort Victoria, the Hudson's Bay Company encouraged settlement and land clearance for agricultural purposes in this area in the 1850s. The peninsula is considered one of the oldest agricultural areas in British Columbia.

The Indigenous Shaker Church, a First Nations church at Brentwood Bay, combines two modest house-like structures, presenting a rather humble appearance. Its generally economical construction concept is consistent with other similar Shaker churches throughout the Pacific Northwest.

The façade on the building to the left is finished in a board-and-batten style, whereas the building on the right has been coated with a stucco finish. Apart from that, the only elements that identify this building as a church are the two large white Christian crosses, certainly indicative of a place of prayer and worship.

Indigenous Shaker Churches, according to historical accounts, represent a unique blend of Coast Salish and Christian beliefs dating to about 1882 and unrelated to the Shaker movement of the eastern U.S. The churches are predominantly located in the coastal regions of Washington state and the southern coast of British Columbia.

REGION - TWO

LOWER MAINLAND &
COAST MOUNTAINS

ST. MARY AND
ST. PAUL

- Lytton –

Almost overnight during the 1850s a gold rush made the small village of Lytton a boom town. Prospectors by the thousands traveled through this area. Some settled in the area, while others headed further north to the Cariboo gold fields and others northeast to Fort Kamloops and beyond.

Lytton is located high up on a plateau above the confluence of the mighty Fraser River and the clear waters of the Thompson River. This is where, in 1808, Simon Fraser named the river formerly called the Sheewap in honour of his friend David Thompson.

At the north end of town is a wonderful early-1900s church that stands above the Thompson River and below the present-day Trans-Canada Highway.

St. Mary and St. Paul Anglican Church is believed to be the second church at this site, the former building having been constructed sometime in the mid- to late 1800s. St. Mary and St. Paul has a blend of architectural elements reminiscent of Gothic, Tudor and modern styles.

The front porch is nicely accented in a Tudor-style trim complete with gable brackets. Above the porch is an exceptional stained-glass commemorative window depicting a visiting priest on horseback on his way to or from a church in the region.

Beneath the front roof façia boards are four large gable brackets, seemingly placed there to enhance the appearance of the main structure. Situated on the roof is a four-posted belfry complete with a classic bell-cast style steeple. The steeple is shingled in the tradition of the period. The roof is covered in a modern asphalt shingle.

On the side of the building are large gothic-style windows customary in old church construction. Near the front corners are wedge-like buttresses, which provide additional wall strength as well as style. In addition, it appears that a series of tie rods have been installed, which is not unusual in older buildings.

At the front of the property, in line with the entrance to the church, is a complex post-and-beam style lych gate, the roofed gateway that is a typical Anglican feature. It was, and perhaps still is, used as a resting place for a coffin before burial.

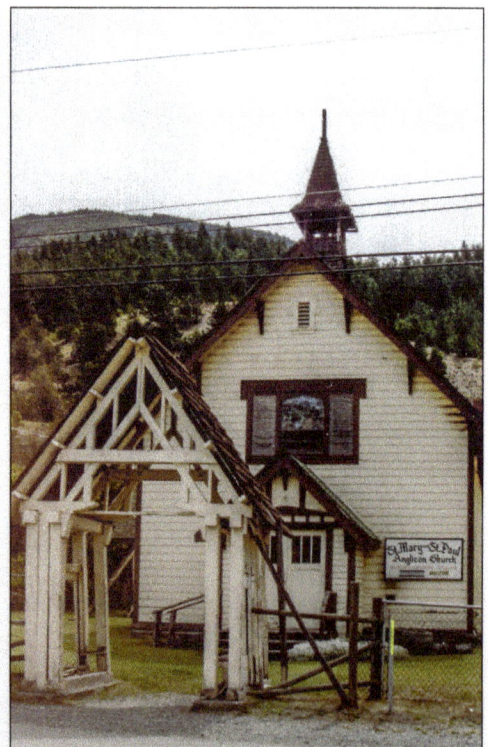

ST. GEORGE'S CHAPEL
- 1906

-Lytton –

At a place originally called "The Forks," appropriately named in 1808 by Simon Fraser, grew the small town of Lytton, the name it was given in the mid-1800s during the Great Gold Rush. Lytton is situated at the junction of the Trans-Canada Highway and the Cariboo Highway, #12. The latter route follows the east bank of the Fraser River along mountainous terrain, connecting with Highway 99 at Lillooet.

Along this route, at about the three-kilometre point just north of Lytton, is a small aboriginal village. At this settlement stands St. George's Anglican Chapel, built in 1906 as part of a First Nations mission.

It is an imposing stone building with numerous bold, interlocking buttresses around its perimeter, an architectural feature that dates to the Middle Ages. Attached to the northwest corner, also constructed of stone, is the sacristy or vestry, the place where a minister or priest prepares for services.

St. George's Chapel is an impressive structure and a testament to the exceptional workmanship of the stone masons who built it.

Local lore imparts the story that the stained-glass windows were removed years ago to preserve the fragile pieces that make up the overall composition of the windows, which were one-of-a-kind historical works of art.

In many aboriginal communities, it has been the practice to remove precious items such as windows once the church or chapel has, for whatever reason, outlived it usefulness. Often, but not always, it was the local congregation that purchased these items.

ST. ANDREW'S CHURCH

- Boothroyd –

About halfway between Hope and Lytton is the famous Fraser Canyon town of Boston Bar, apparently named after several American prospectors who came from Boston in search of gold on nearby sandbars, locally referred to as "the men from Boston."

A few miles north of Boston Bar is the Boothroyd First Nation, a quiet, humble community situated adjacent to the Trans-Canada Highway.

The church there, called St. Andrew's Anglican, is constructed from logs of a modern design, an architectural type that dates to about 1948. This new construction method is of the Pan Abode design. Rough-cut rectangular logs are put through a machine molder that creates a double tongue-and-groove profile. Near the ends of these molded logs are specially cut notches that allow each log to tightly interlock with another.

Pan Abode buildings are manufactured in kit form and are easily erected at a designated site of choice, skilled labour not required.

The belfry is quite simple but fitting for a church of this design. The multi-pane windows, while not equal in size or number of panes, are also relative to the overall composition of this modest building.

Simple design, low mainte-nance and functionality are key elements of a long-lasting structure.

ST. JOSEPH'S CHURCH
- 1880

- Yale –

Once the 1846 border question between Canada and the United States was settled, the Hudson's Bay Company developed an alternate route that took the Hudson's Bay Company horse brigades from Fort Kamloops to Fort Yale, a route that proved to be very treacherous. The trail through the Fraser Canyon led to huge losses in terms of furs and packhorses, and the route was quickly abandoned. Another route was found through the Coquihalla Mountain region, which terminated at Fort Hope.

By 1850, gold was discovered in the north country, and in 1858 Governor James Douglas ordered that town plans be made at Fort Yale. In 1860, Charles Grandidier, an Oblate Father, established a Catholic mission at Fort Yale.

Three years later, the Cariboo Wagon Road between Fort Yale and Cook's Ferry to the north (now called Spence's Bridge) was nearing completion. HBC operations at Fort Yale closed in 1892.

Twelve years before the closure of the HBC post, St. Joseph's Catholic Church was built. It is a rather ordinary structure, with a single entrance door in the tower and a rectangular window above. Higher up the tower is a small, plain, spoke-wheel window. The tower is capped by a pyramid-style roof and cross.

The three side windows are also of simple design. Overall, this 129-year-old church is in remarkable shape, considering the wet climate in the area.

Obviously, the care and attention given by local residents throughout the generations has had an impact on its survival.

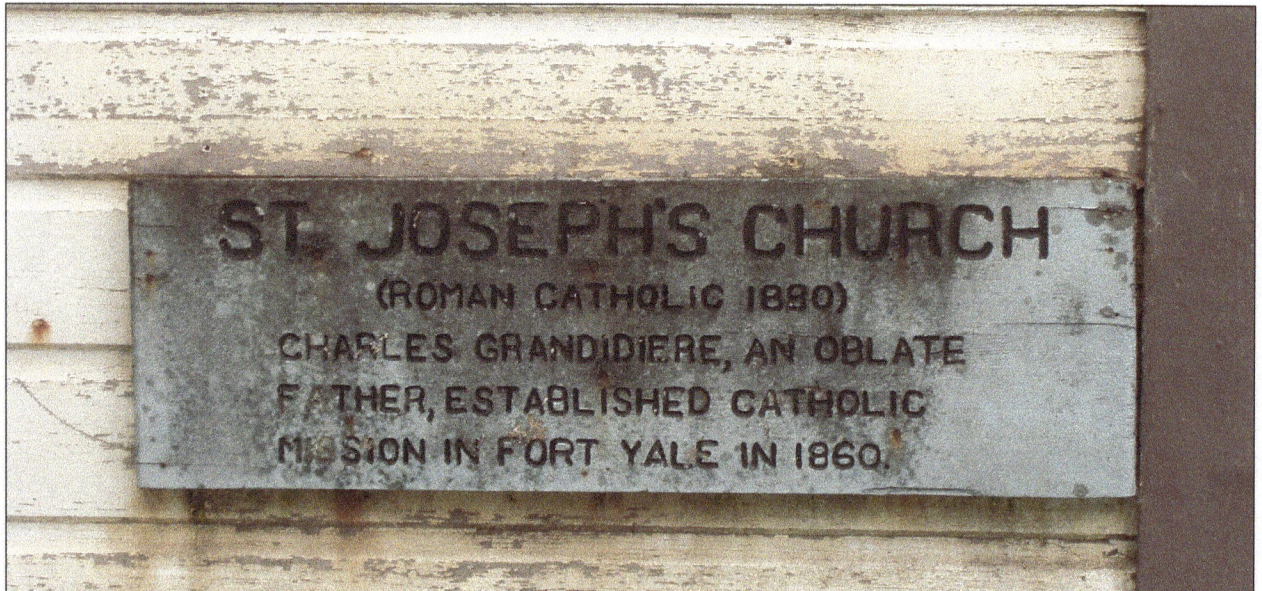

ST. CHRISTOPHER'S CHURCH

- *Mount Currie* –

At the base of Mount Currie lie the arable lands of the Pemberton Valley, the heartland of the Mount Currie band, now known as the Lil'wat First Nation people. This area was also part of the Douglas Gold Trail, which gold-seekers of long ago plodded along as they headed north to Port Anderson, now called D'Arcy.

Near the junction of Highway 99 and Pemberton Meadows Road stands an impressive Roman Catholic edifice by the name of St. Christopher's Church.

It is a typical rectangular structure with a steep-pitched metal roof. Attached to the main body of the church is a small covered porch of a similar roof pitch configuration. On the roof is a delightful belfry and cross feature.

The side walls have three timbered buttress assemblies, suggesting possible structural difficulties at one time in its recent past. Between these buttresses are three regular-size pointed windows.

While not an overpowering structure and by all measures conventional in design, this church is inviting to the onlooker.

CHURCH OF THE HOLY CROSS
- 1895

- Skookumchuck –

During the 1858 Barkerville Gold Rush in the Cariboo, James Douglas, and HBC fur trader and governor of British Columbia, established the famous "Douglas Gold Trail," also known as the Lakes Route. It was an alternate inland route to the Cariboo that originated at Fort Langley, then proceeded up the Fraser and Harrison Rivers and beyond, over a series of lakes and portages, to Cayoosh Flat. The Harrison, Lillooet, Anderson and Seaton lakes formed part of this great route to the Interior, effectively bypassing the Fraser Canyon. After a well-deserved rest, the miners, speculators and entrepreneurs would set off once again, this time over the Cariboo Wagon Road to Soda Creek at the Fraser River. Here, these travelers essentially ended the second leg of their journey to the gold fields.

The name Cayoosh Flat was changed a few years later to Lillooet, a name apparently more fitting for the new frontier gentry of the day. Almost

literally overnight, this bustling town became a major transportation hub connecting traffic from the Harrison route to the Cariboo Wagon Road. It was designated mile zero, as a reference point for the many roadhouses along the way to the gold fields.

About 20 miles along the Douglas Trail, just north of Port Douglas on Harrison Lake, is a place called Skookumchuck, a Chinook Jargon word meaning rapid waters. Situated here between

the Douglas Trail and the Lillooet River is a small aboriginal community and a stately triple-spire Roman Catholic church by the name of Church of the Holy Cross.

The Carpenter Gothic-style architecture is exceptional and beautiful in every detail, a one-of-a-kind structure not replicated anywhere in British Columbia.

From the awesome exterior towers and soaring spires to the elaborate decorative elements, this structure is an expression of profound and complex design rarely seen in a wooden church of this period. It was indeed a commendable undertaking by local artisans at the time of its construction.

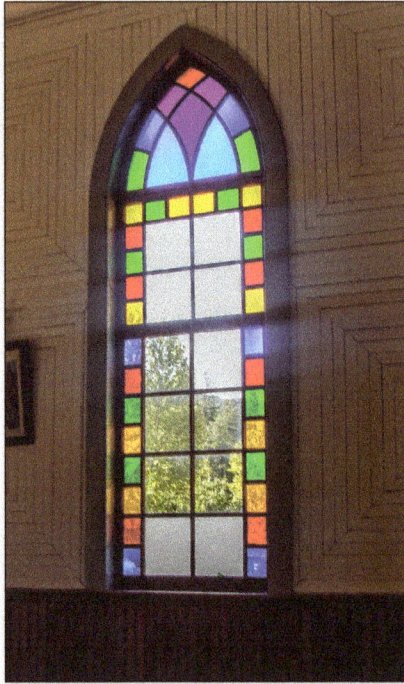

The handcrafted altar embodies elements of the three spires, supported by a colonnade base, richly embellished. Delicately turned balusters complete the balustrade that separates the sanctuary from the nave. Two confessionals flank the front doors at each corner, a format not often seen in frontier-style churches.

The stained-glass windows were purchased from Europe and paid for through community donations; they are exemplary works of art fitting for a church of this caliber.

In 1981, the Church of the Holy Cross was designated a Canadian National Heritage Site.

This church is truly a jewel in the wilderness, completely intact and waiting for the next generation to keep safe its delicate structure for those yet to come.

SACRED HEART
- 1926

- Chawathil – Hope –

On a large flatland area near the base of Dog Mountain is the community of Chawathil. This community is tucked away in the northeast Cascade Mountain region of the Fraser Valley. The land is partly divided by Highway 7 and the Canadian Pacific Railway.

Sacred Heart Church occupies a prominent position at the entrance to the community and appears well cared for and reasonably maintained for a wooden structure of its age.

At first glance, one is drawn to the large, square bell tower to the right of the building, a style reminiscent of other churches of this period. The entrance to the church has a very nice covered porch and a lovely, open archway that is modestly detailed.

All the windows are in the gothic style, including the doubled, louvered openings near the top of the tower. The main structure of this Catholic church is quite large, enough to support a sizable congregation. A plain white cross adorns the rooftop near the front gable.

The people here are most courteous and respectful when engaged in conversation about their church.

IMMACULATE CONCEPTION

- Seabird Island – Agassiz –

A few miles west of the community of Chawathil on Highway 7 is the First Nation village of Seabird Island. The island is separated by the Fraser River on the southeast side and the Maria Slough to the northwest. The island was named after the paddle-wheeler Sea Bird, which, according to historical accounts, ran aground on the island in 1858.

The residents of Seabird Island are very industrious and business-oriented. For many, many decades, travelers passing through this part of the country have been stopping in at the Sea Bird Restaurant, gas bar and convenience store.

Agricultural pursuits such as orchards, farming and other ventures provide worthwhile opportunities, and there is a progressive attitude here that will serve the First Nation well and the generations that follow.

The church, Immaculate Conception, is constructed primarily from modern concrete cinder block; it is a large, squat-looking building of modest design. The façade is rather unembellished except for a small cross mounted at the apex of the gable. Windows are clear rectangular-pane assemblies that allow a good deal of light to enter the structure.

Architecturally, the only element of note is a stand-alone cross-like cinder block column that supports an open four-posted platform and roof to house the church bell. Apart from that, the exterior of the building is in pretty good shape.

ST. MICHAEL'S

- Ohamil – Laidlaw –

Deep in the upper reaches of the Fraser Valley, near the settlement of Laidlaw, is a small community by the name of Ohamil, home of the Shxwowhamel First Nation. It is along St. Elmo Road, once known as Old Yale Road. The original road was built in the late 1870s and meandered through the valley, following the southeast bank of the Fraser River.

Within the community stands a charming Roman Catholic church, St. Michael's. While somewhat weather-beaten and in need of attention, it has miraculously survived rather well for its age.

The style of this building is of the late 1890s to early 1900s, a simple design that incorporates a typical square bell tower and front entrance. It has pointed, arched windows often seen in churches of this period.

On the west side of the church, near the back, is a side door sheltered by what appears to be a shed-like porch; it's a nice touch that blends in remarkably well with the overall design.

Considering the harsh seasons in this mountainous region, the local residents have so far managed to preserve their church with a level of zeal that is commendable, to say the least.

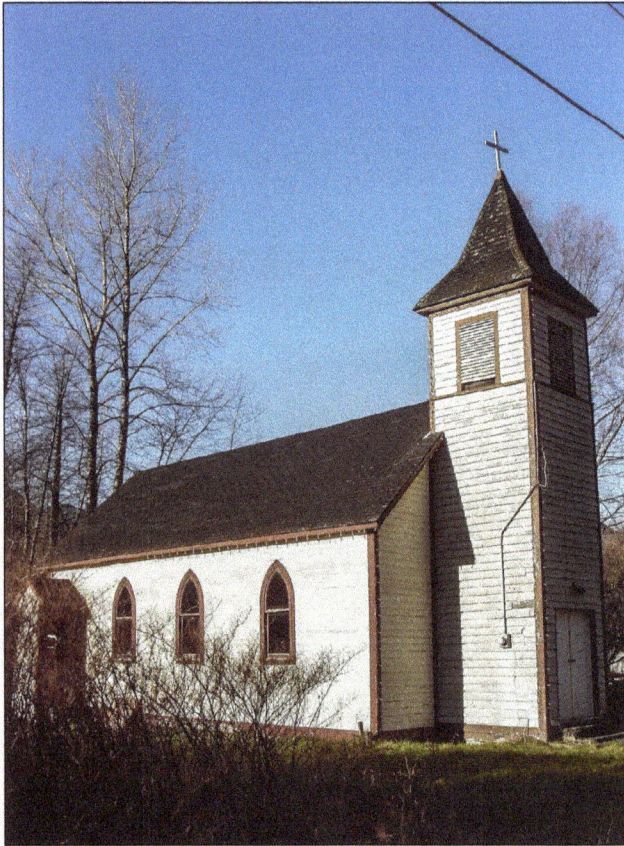

CHURCH OF THE HOLY GHOST
- 1904

- Tsawwassen -

The ancient aboriginal village of Tsawwassen dates back more than 4,000 years and overlooks the southern Strait of Georgia and the lower Fraser River. The Strait, part of the Salish Sea, was named by Captain George Vancouver in 1792.

The original Catholic church in this community was dedicated as the Church of the Holy Ghost in 1904. This church is a simple, rudimentary, one-floor rectangular building with a steep, gabled roof.

The exterior was finished with rough-cut horizontal clapboard siding and detailed with three gothic-style wooden windows on each side of the building. A covered porch entrance to the inner church doors completes the basic architectural design.

Sometime after 1930, the old church was replaced with a more modern church, which today stands in apparent abandonment. This church of the same name incorporates more architectural elements, while having a similar rectangular footprint. It includes a small, stepped-down enclosed porch entrance with double swinging front doors embellished with white crosses.

The church displays seven gothic-style windows on each side of the main church structure, as well as one window in the same style on each side of the porch. A short, square bell tower, complete with multiple louvered vents on each side, is capped by a four-sided, steep-pitched roof supporting a single cross.

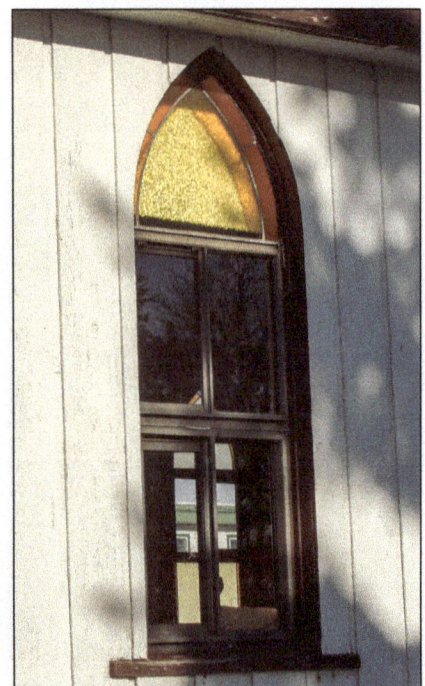

ST. ANNE'S

- Semiahmoo – White Rock –

Southeast of White Rock, off the shores of Semiahmoo Bay and just north of the International Boundary, is the village of the Semiahmoo First Nation. The village is situated along the shoreline between the border crossing and Campbell River; it's a quiet and peaceful area that overlooks the Strait of Georgia and the Gulf Islands.

In a heavily treed setting is St. Anne's Catholic Church, a building of modern design and materials. The floor plan is essentially a one-storey building with two small structures added on, one at each end. A short bell tower and bell-cast style roof and cross assembly is positioned on the rooftop towards the front entrance.

The church has a small porch at the entrance and a very large deck to the side, presumably used for large gatherings.

On the whole, this church is meticulously looked after and is one of the most inviting and delightful little churches anywhere in the region.

INDIGENOUS SHAKER CHURCH
- 1997

- North Vancouver –

The congregations of most Indigenous Shaker churches in the southern coastal waters of British Columbia are generally descendants of Coast Salish people. Shaker Churches extend south across the border into Washington state and elsewhere along the Pacific Coast.

The church at Capilano is a new, quasi-modern building, especially the front entrance area. The porch has a nice low-pitched roof supported by large vertical and sloped timbers, complete with bolted horizontal cross members. The front wall, with its four slender windows next to the front doors, gently slopes in the opposite direction to the roof line, emphasizing the overall design.

The exterior walls are finished in a typical board-and-batten form that is characteristic of old frontier construction.

CHURCH OF THE REDEEMER
- 1897

- Kwantlin – McMillan Island –

A small island in the lower Fraser River is named McMillan, after James McMillan, once Chief Factor of the Hudson's Bay Company. McMillan led some of the first surveys of the area and established the original Fort Langley in 1827 at a place called Derby. In 1839 the fort was moved further upriver, adjacent to McMillan Island.

McMillan Island is the home of the Kwantlen First Nation and to the Church of the Redeemer.

The façade of this tall, narrow, uncomplicated Roman Catholic church is well preserved and conventional in design. Over the top of the front doors is a triangular-style window, and above that a small spoke-wheel window. On both sides of the church are three pointed stained-glass windows. The structure is completed by a rather modest, louvered bell tower and cross.

This lovely old island church has been designated a Historic Site by the Township of Langley.

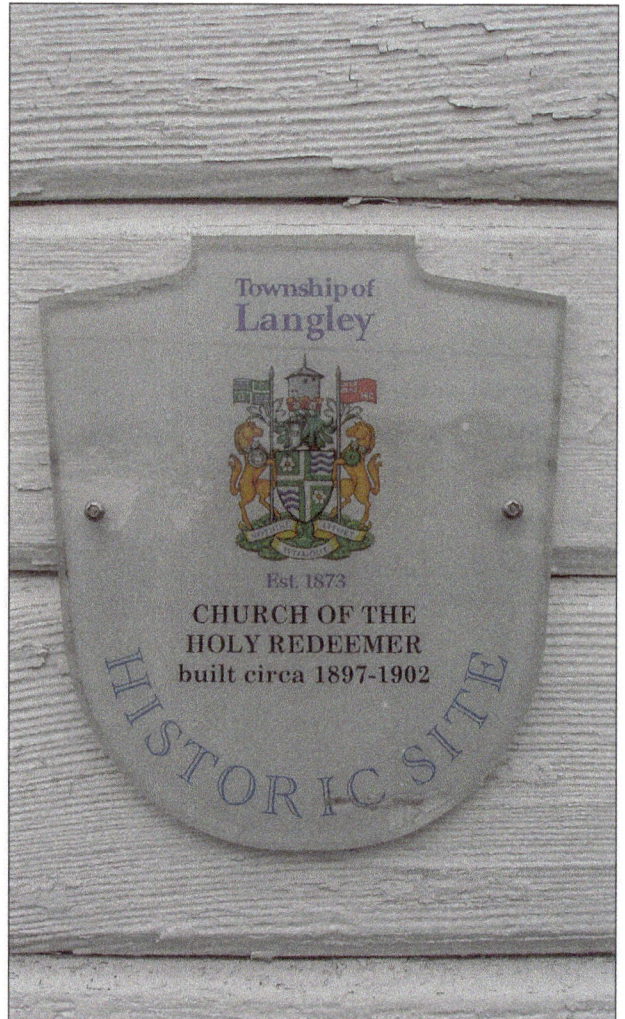

Township of
Langley

Est. 1873

CHURCH OF THE
HOLY REDEEMER
built circa 1897-1902

HISTORIC SITE

ST. MARY MAGDALEN

- Cheam – Rosedale –

As one enters the Bridal Veil Falls area from the east, the land along the left side of the highway begins to ascend fairly quickly to the upper reaches of the mountains above. Cheam Peak, the dominant peak in the area, rises to about 6,800 feet above the Cheam Lake wetlands and the farmlands of Rosedale.

Not far from the junction of the Trans-Canada Highway and Highway 9 is the Cheam First Nation community. Situated close to the administration building is the Roman Catholic church of St. Mary Magdalen. It is a large, squat, unassuming structure, simple in design and somewhat deficient in special architectural elements.

The façade has a low-pitched roof and a slightly curved, cantilevered roof over a pair of plain slab-type doors. Above this roof is a very modest multiblock window in the form of a cross. The exterior walls of the church are completely clad in cedar shingles.

This uncomplicated example of church architecture is unique in the region.

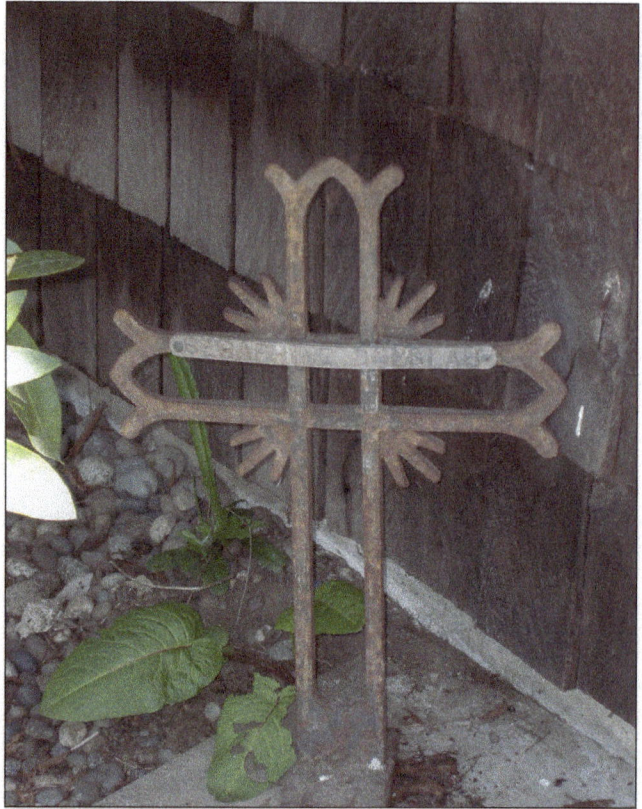

ST. TERESA'S

- Yakweakwioose – Sardis –

In the heartlands of the Upper Fraser Valley lie vast tracts of fertile agricultural land in and around the small community of Sardis. In addition to agricultural activities, there are dairy farms and numerous industrial enterprises in the region. Sardis is also the home of the Yakweakwioose First Nation and St. Teresa's Catholic Church.

St. Teresa's is a small house-like structure with beveled clapboard siding, double entrance doors and gothic arched windows. Over the front doors is a plain shed-style roof. The belfry has obviously seen better times. It appears there may have been an enclosure of some sort applied to the open framework beneath its roof.

On top of the pediment-style roof is a short cone-shaped spire complete with a large cross. The general appearance of St. Teresa's Church is rather elementary but nonetheless eye-catching.

OUR LADY OF FATIMA

- *Chehalis* –

Throughout the mountains, rivers and lakes of the Harrison Mills area, so legend purports, lurks the legendary Sasquatch, a human-like creature that stalks the local forests and rivers of the Harrison and Chehalis. This area saw thousands of gold-seekers making their way along the Harrison River by paddle-wheeler in the 1850s, a famous route that took them to Port Douglas and beyond via several portage and lake systems to Lillooet.

At the outfall of the Chehalis River, where it meets the Harrison, is the land of the Chehalis First Nation. The community is very progressive and supports an infrastructure equal to that of many small towns in the region. Among the many buildings and homes is a relatively new church that appears to have been built within the last few decades.

Our Lady of Fatima Catholic Church is not a typical church design. It's more along the lines of a prefabricated modular structure that was perhaps converted. The exterior, while humble in a conventional way, does have an outstanding quality about it.

However, the interior is very much a church, a place where one instantly disconnects with the outside environment. The altar is attractive, tastefully constructed and designed to complement the angular form of the ceiling. The walls and furnishings are lightly accented in a pleasant native motif, a delightful expression and sense of identity.

In the right front corner of the sanctuary stands a Talking Stick, a democratic symbol used in many West Coast aboriginal cultures. When it's in the possession of a speaker, it is considered impolite to interrupt or raise objections to what's being said until the carved wooden staff is passed on to another person. The person who receives the stick then has the opportunity for rebuttal or can move on to another subject. The stick is generally carved with various clan symbols, the most predominant of which are the eagle or thunderbird.

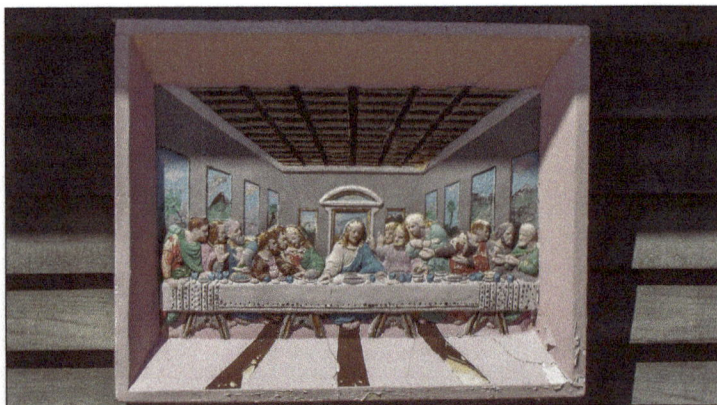

Other traditional church elements are also presented in the customary way according to the Catholic tradition.

ST. MICHAEL THE ARCHANGEL

- Musqueam – Vancouver –

Musqueam is southwest of Vancouver proper and along the shoreline of the north arm of the Fraser River, directly across from Iona Island. Today the island is connected to Sea Island by a causeway.

Oral history explains how the name Musqueam came about. Apparently the name of the grass along the shoreline was translated by early inhabitants as musqueam. Thus the local people are the People of the River Grass.

Within this enterprising community stands the second church to occupy these lands. The first was built around 1902 and subsequently destroyed in a storm or a fire. The new church, however, is a large wooden structure of modern design with a rather plain façade and a large flat cross above the entrance.

At the left front corner stands a rough-built tower with a single entry door. The top of the tower is an open four-posted belfry complete with a pyramid-style roof. Below the bell is a statue of St. Michael the Archangel slaying the hosts of evil.

In the original 1902 church, the statue of St. Michael the Archangel was placed over the front doors in a semi-enclosed niche, a focal point of the church, which had extraordinary twin towers and spires that rivaled those at the Church of the Holy Cross at Skookumchuck.

ST. PAUL'S INDIGENOUS CHURCH
- 1884

- North Vancouver -

St. Paul's Indigenous Church, the pride of the Squamish First Nation, is the third church built since 1863 at a place called Ustlawn Village.

In 1909, the church was substantially remodeled; the old bell tower was replaced by twin towers, and there were other external and internal alterations.

By 1980, major restoration plans were once again underway. This time it was transformed into the grand structure we witness today, the results of a restoration completed by Christmas 1983.

This church is an excellent example of gothic style. The towers are deeply set into the façade and supported with decorative buttresses on all corners. The towers combine two double sets of doors that are pleasantly trimmed on each side with dual columns, topped with an elaborate fretwork-style pediment. The steeples are covered in sheet metal and adorned with a series of dormers of various sizes.

Between the towers is a classic 12-petal rosette window. On the west lawn the original 1881 church bell is displayed.

The floor plan of the church is in the cruciform design. The interior arches are tastefully highlighted in a distinctive Coast Salish motif, very attractive and relevant to

the church's heritage. The walls, vaulted ceiling and pews are painted white, providing a nice balance to the finished woodwork throughout.

During the time of this immense project, St. Paul's Church was designated a National Heritage Site. St. Paul's has stood proudly overlooking Burrard Inlet on the north shore for well over a century. On a clear day the mountain peaks called the Lions can be seen in the background as one looks skyward through the twin steeples a short distance away.

At night, the large crosses that adorn the two towers are illuminated and can be seen from far and wide. During the early days of the mission the church often served as a navigational aid to ships that entered the harbour. Today the area is home to the Mosquito Creek Marina and other commercial enterprises.

This charming old church is believed to be the second church at the Ustlawn Squamish settlement on the North Shore of Burrard Inlet.

St. Paul's Indigenous, 1864
Photo courtesy of North Shore
Musuem & Archives

ST. MARY'S CHURCH
- 1870'S

– Slosh Indian Reserve – Seton Lake West End –

Near this Reserve is the famous Seaton Lake Portage that connects to Anderson Lake It was the final leg of the 1858 inland trek that brought the would be gold miners, merchants and speculators to this region.

Packs, bags and whatever they could muster were transported over the three mile Portage by a horse drawn railway cart from Anderson Lake. From this point the trekkers made there way down Seton Lake to Cayoosh Flats. (Lillooet)

Close to this embarkation point is, St. Mary's Church presumably built in the 1870's. This church has been left to decay and will soon vanish from the landscape.

However, before this happens, there are a few architectural elements worth mentioning. The main structure is constructed with square hewn logs with perfect squared off dove tail corners. The log façade has been completely covered with clapboards, while the side walls have been left exposed.

The covered porch still has the original two panel door with arched frame work at the top. Above the door is a rectangular transom style window. Both sides of the church have lovely Gothic arched windows. The six open posted belfry supports a six sided steeple with a turned wooden sphere

and cross. The steeple is finished with small square cut shingles around the perimeter of the bottom section, diamond shape shingles up to the mid point and back again to square cut shingles to the top. An exceptional piece of carpentry work not often emulated.

St. Mary's Church is an original frontier log structure that clearly demonstrates a high degree of craftsmanship by local inhabitants of past generations. There artistic designs and over all structural composition is definitely a legacy to be passed on, whether by hands on teaching or through pictures.

St. Mary's Church, 20XX

St. Mary's Church, 1969.
Photo from *Old Wooden Buildings*, Hancock House, 1978

INFANT JESUS OF PRAGUE

- Burrard – Dollarton Highway –

In 1792 Captain George Vancouver surveyed a large arm shaped fiord and named it Burrards Canal after his friend Sr. Harry Burrard. Years later the west arm of the canal was renamed Burrard Inlet, and the north arm, renamed Indian Arm. Presumably because the Indian River flows into the north end of this body of water.

At the base of Mount Seymour and along the shore line between the Second Narrows Bridge, now called, Iron Workers Memorial Bridge, and the point of land called Roche Point, is the community of the Burrard Band. The land there is essentially split into two sections by the Dollarton Highway. Along this road stands a beautiful little Catholic Church by the name, Infant Jesus of Prague.

The structure is a basic two level rectangular building with a covered in porch, above the double doors is a glass enclosed niche with a statue that appears to be a likeness of a robed priest with crown. Flanking the porch are two small wide arched windows.

At the west front corner of the church is what seems to be an addition that was built on years later. Above the addition is a short small square tower, toped with a tapering four sided steeple and cross. On the east side of the building is a shrine that is elaborately adorned with various figurines on the front corner posts. The main feature is a large six foot statue of the Virgin Mary.

The Church of the Infant Jesus of Praque is an outstanding structure, it is well kept and refreshing clean, neat and tidy. Clearly a sacred place for worship.

ST. MARY'S CHURCH
- 1890's

- Nkiat – Seton Portage –

Local oral history says a catastrophic event took place here thousands of years ago, when a huge rock slide of a monumental scale crashed down at a place about the midpoint of a large lake. The slide literally split the lake into two bodies of water, forming a massive land bridge. Evidence of this event can be seen on the south face of the mountain range.

In the late 1840s this land bridge became known as the Portage, then many decades later Seton Portage.

The southern lake was named after A.C. Anderson, a Hudson's Bay Company fur trader and explorer in this region, and the northern lake was named Seton Lake after a close relative of Anderson.

After the famous 1858 Cariboo Gold Rush, a second gold strike was declared in the late 1890s at a place called Bridge River. Gold-seekers of this period also used the Seton Portage route. As the miners made their way up Anderson Lake by steamboat they soon reached the south end of Seton Portage and the village of Nkiat. It is believed they passed by St. Mary's Church on their way to the north end of the portage.

Once they reached the north end, they traveled by foot, hauling their worldly possessions on pack horses or mules along a trail on the north side of Seton Lake to another village, Shalath. From there they turned left and began the difficult task of ascending a treacherous mountain trail with dozens of switchbacks until they reached the Mission Mountain Pass. They then descended down an equally dangerous trail to the valley below, to Bridge River. Today this 5,000-foot pass trail is called Mission Mountain Road; it possesses what's considered the steepest road grade in B.C.

St. Mary's Church is in fairly good condition for a church of this age. The main building is short in length with only two arched windows on each side; there is also a small addition to the rear.

The façade is unique. Above the double entrance doors, the façade is completed with a full-width porch roof and veranda.

The church has a large tower with large, clear-glass windows on three sides of the upper half. The top of the tower supports a low upward-slanting roof and a multi open-arched posted drum. On top of the drum is a three-segmented steeple, each segment finished in scalloped shingles, except for the midsection, where it appears the shingles have succumbed to harsh weather. At the apex of the steeple is a large turned sphere and decorative cross with a four-pointed star.

Services are held here on a regular basis when weather and road conditions permit.

HOLY ROSARY CHURCH
- 1910's

- D'Arcy -

The community of D'Arcy was formerly known as Port Anderson, a port that once bustled with wild excitement as thousands of would-be gold seekers arrived after a long and difficult trip over the Douglas Gold Trail. At this point, the final leg of the trip to Cayoosh Flats (Lillooet) was not far off.

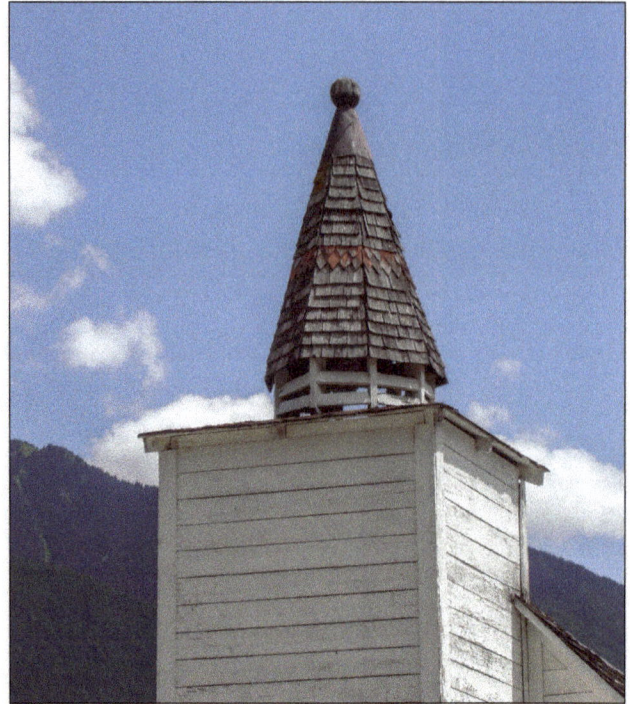

After the decline of the gold rush, Port Anderson gradually faded away as a port of any significance. This wilderness area basically reverted almost entirely to a First Nation settlement. The village was renamed D'Arcy, evidently after a railway worker of the Pacific Great Eastern Railway, which came through this region.

Holy Rosary Church is characteristically a frontier-style structure. It has a simple, box-like tower and a relatively flat roof that loosely supports a drum and steeple. The steeple appears to be sinking into the tower after decades of decay around the base of the drum. At the entranceway, there are obvious signs of reconstruction, where at one time there were probably two doors and not one, as we see now.

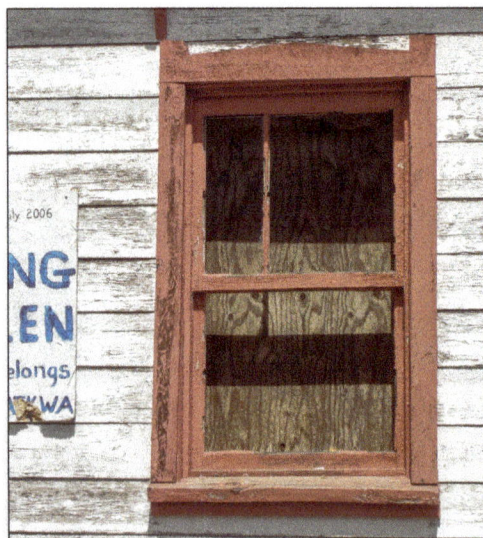

Under the eaves is a series of hand-cut brackets, a respectable embellishment. The side windows are crudely framed and in a state of disrepair. The pediment-like design at the top of the frame is rather awkward-looking.

Major restoration work is needed to bring this once charming and appealing Catholic church building back to its original standard. In the past several decades, there has been a restoration revival throughout British Columbia, a noble and worthwhile effort for the benefit of future generations.

SACRED HEART CHURCH
- 1900's

- Sliammon – Powell River –

About six miles north of Powell River on the Sunshine Coast is the First Nations community of Sliammon. The site is on a sandy shoreline overlooking Harwood Island in the picturesque Malaspina Strait.

Local information briefly states that a Catholic church was built there in 1896. In the early 1900s, the first Sacred Heart was destroyed by fire, then quickly rebuilt by the local residents. The result of this undertaking is the church we see today.

It is a first-class building in every sense. The three-section square tower is deeply set into the main structure, incorporating a single front door. Above the door is a fan-shaped window. Near the top of the first section is a large, eight-petal circular window.

The second section has a lovely, rounded-arch niche, complete with a statue that was miraculously retrieved from the fire that destroyed the former church. The third and final section, which houses the church bell, has two louvered, arched openings on each side. A pyramid-style roof with returned eaves completes all three sections.

Flanking the front door are two rounded-arch windows, a style that is carried through to the sides of the church. The rounded arch design theme is a dominate element throughout this building.

The people at Sacred Heart are very friendly and helpful, with an impressive knowledge of their church.

OUR LADY OF LOURDES

- Sechelt –

Sechelt is a First Nations name meaning land between two waters, according to the local residents. Sechelt is located on a narrow piece of land, with its shores being on the Sechelt Inlet to the north and the Strait of Georgia on the south. Basically, it's a land bridge that, if washed away, would separate the Sechelt Peninsula from the mainland.

According to a member of the Catholic parish, there has been a church on the Sechelt Reserve since about 1868. The previous one built on this site was destroyed by fire in 1971. Around 1973 a new building located at the Royal Canadian Air Force base in Ladner was towed across the Strait of Georgia to Sechelt to became the second Catholic church named Our Lady of Lourdes.

This new church is set back a few hundred yards from the southern shore, where beautiful sandy beaches provide a place of contentment and magnificent ocean views. The building is a nice structure and complements the surrounding area well. The west side features a series of eight arched windows. A small four-posted belfry and large cross adorn the façade.

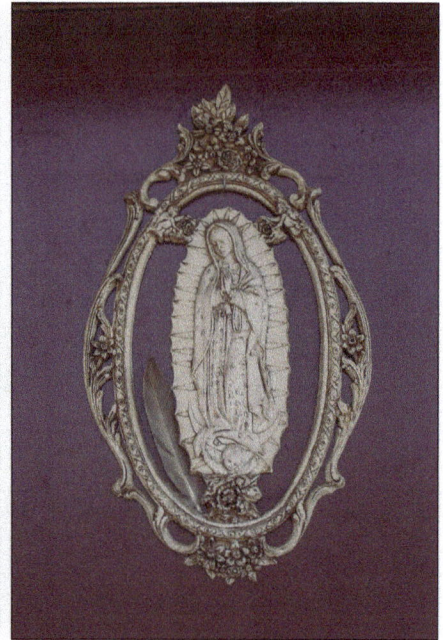

The priest's living quarters are attached to the east side of the church and finished in the same style as the main building. On the front door is a large, exquisite silver medallion depicting the Virgin Mary.

Upon entering the church one feels an immediate disconnect with the outside world. It is indeed an awesome experience. The décor is warm and welcoming. In the sanctuary area is a formal altar placed close to the back wall. Above it are three red, arched window-like panels, flanked by two eye-catching wall hangings with an indigenous theme. On the far left is a striking lectern with delicately carved panels, topped by a hand-carved eagle with wings spread out to support the Bible.

REGION - THREE

THOMPSON OKANAGAN

ST. JOSEPH'S
· 1870

Kamloops

Located between the grand landmark mountain peaks of Paul and Peter and Battle Bluff, which offers outstanding views of Kamloops Lake, is a beautiful city called Kamloops. It stands at the point where the North and South Thompson Rivers converge. The city was founded in 1812 in the area then known by the Shuswap people as Tk'eml'ups. The Shuswap have lived along the rivers and lakes of this area for thousands of years.

Battle Bluff is one of the most prominent hills along the north shore of Kamloops Lake, a short distance from the old site of the Tranquille tuberculosis hospital. According to Benjamin Baltzly, who visited and photographed the area in 1871, the name Battle Bluff was derived from an indigenous legend about a skirmish that took place on the waters just below the promontory a century earlier.

To the east, Mounts Paul and Peter form an impressive backdrop to the city below and are perhaps the most remarkable features in the immediate area. The mountain peaks also memorialize two notable First Nations chiefs who had been nicknamed St. Paul and St. Peter.

St. Paul, properly known as Chief Lolo, was well respected by his people and the fur traders of the period; it seems that he would preach the good word to everyone he came in contact with.

St. Peter was the nickname given to a widely known chief by the name of Tenemasket who had been dubbed Peter by local traders, whom he visited frequently with a good haul of furs. He was likewise seemingly recognized as a good man. Both chiefs reportedly maintained strong leadership within their own communities and served as intermediaries with the fur traders. With the arrival of European settlers in 1812, Kamloops ultimately became the main transportation hub for the south-central Interior. The North West Company built its first fur-trading fort on the east side of the river junction, later part of the Hudson's Bay Company. Years later, this site became one of the reserves of the Kamloops Band —Tk'eml'ups te Secwepemc.

Situated not far from the base of Mount Paul stands St. Joseph's Catholic Church, now a heritage building. The first church here was established in 1870 and was built of logs by Catholic missionaries and band members. After undergoing several alterations before the turn of the last century, the old church was torn down to make way for a new frame church, in a cruciform-style floor plan. Photographs in the Kamloops Band brochure show that the bell tower was apparently rescued from the old building and reused in the new church; St. Joseph's Church was restored in 1985 by the band.

The interior of this wonderful old church is in exceptional condition and obviously well cared for. It is filled with an overwhelming level of elegance and beauty. Upon entering the church, one's eyes are immediately drawn to the sanctuary, where a massive white and gold-trimmed altar stands. The church features a multitude of ornamental details, columns and statues.

Flanking the handsome, solid-wood pews are exquisitely handcrafted frames that elaborately showcase handpainted plaster-cast depictions of the Stations of the Cross. St. Joseph's Church is truly an impressive historic jewel within this First Nations community.

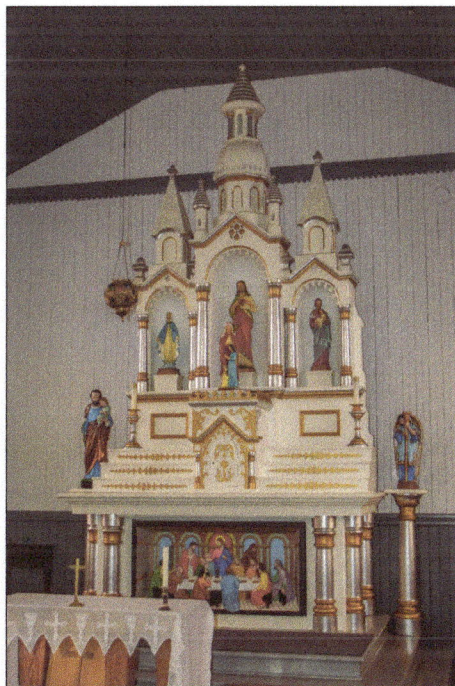

ST JOHN THE BAPTIST

Chu Chua

On the flats at Tsegurtsegweig, north of Kamloops on the North Thompson River, was the original community of the Simpcw First Nation, formerly known as the North Thompson Band. In about 1900, a small chapel was built there. In 1911 the entire community was forced to move to higher ground at a place called Chu Chua, due to frequent flooding and severe river bank erosion.

By the fall of the same year, a plan for a new church finally became a reality, through the donation of many hours of community labour. The building was constructed with new material, save for the bell that was rescued from the original chapel.

In about 1935 a new foundation was added, and in the early 1960s further improvements were made to the interior. The church was again renovated in 1981 and a new heating stove was installed. On October 9, 1995, Thanksgiving Day, the valley's oldest functioning church building was reduced to ashes and rubble.

Soon after this catastrophic event, a new church was built on the same site. The community, as always, remained determined to forge ahead in the traditions that had been established more than a hundred years previous. The new church as it stands today is a modern structure, simple in design, functional and efficient.

Large double glass entrance doors, flanked by long, narrow side windows, offer a welcoming feeling when entering the building. The use of natural

light throughout the entire structure seems to be the general theme. Several skylights were incorporated into the roof design. In addition, the back wall of the building is composed of five contemporary, multi-coloured sectional windows, of which three are embellished with large crosses. Obviously, determination, independence and a strong desire to succeed have given this community the drive necessary to surmount all challenges put before them.

St. John the Baptist, April 2019

St. John the Baptist, 1930s.
Photo from *Royal BC Archives*

St. John the Baptist, 1960s.
Photo from *Diocese of Kamloops*

ST. MARY'S
- 1909

Skeetchestn – Deadman Valley

A few miles west of the town of Savona is a beautiful desert-like valley, rich with legends and myths. Ancient volcanic rock and ash are present throughout the area. Hoodoos, unique split-rock formations, cactus and wild flowers abound in this place, known as Deadman Valley.

Located at the head of the valley is the spectacular Deadman Falls, which closely resembles but is smaller than the famous Helmcken Falls in Wells Gray Park, north of Kamloops. Extreme caution should be used at all times when approaching the undermined outer edges of the landscape around the falls; there are no safety fences there. Downstream from the falls is a series of first-class fishing lakes such as Viadette, Skookum, Snowoosh and Mowich.

From this area, Deadman's Creek meanders through the sprawling ranchlands of the valley below, which embody the ethos of early western settlers. During the 1800s, the fur brigades once traveled trails that paralled the creek through the southern half of the valley as they plodded their way through to Fort Kamloops.

The legend of Deadman's Creek seems to have originated in 1817, when Pierre Charette, of the North West Company, was killed by his travelling companion in a quarrel over a campsite. In 1828, another NWC man called it the Chivrette River. Samuel Black called it the Knife River in 1835, but soon after that it achieved its present designation.

This valley is perhaps the region's most captivating attraction, given its importance to First Nations people, fur traders and cowboys of the old west. Near the south end of the valley, close to the Trans-Canada Highway, is the Skeetchestn First Nation, formerly known as the Deadman Creek Band. Within this prosperous community stands St. Mary's Catholic Church,

constructed in 1909 by band members under the direction of the Oblate missionary Father Jean-Marie-Raphaël Le Jeune.

St. Mary's underwent major restoration and was completed by the band's carpentry crew in 1995. It is used for funerals, weddings, christenings and special masses. This lovely, preserved church, complete with its groomed lawn area, presents very well. On the same grounds is a memorial cairn commemorating the sacrifice made by its members during the wars, a fitting tribute by the community.

ST. LOUIS CHURCH

Cache Creek

They named it Cache Creek in the 1800s. Today, it is a place where the Trans-Canada Highway and Highway 97 meet. The Bonaparte River runs through this town, where ancient aboriginal trails from the north, south and west intersected. The old trails have long since given way to wagon roads and modern paved highways.

Fur traders of the early 1800s were guided through Cache Creek. Samuel Black's 1835 map of the region noted the trail was used before the discovery of gold there. His map probably marked this as the collection point for furs that were bound for the Thompson River post, also

known as Fort Kamloops, when French was the primary traders' language. Cache is a French word for a hiding place or a place to store or accumulate goods—in this sense, a place to store furs. There are various stories about how this place got its name, but this interpretation seems the most likely.

Another interesting name in this area is that of the Bonaparte River, which appears on Archibald McDonald's 1827 map. The river was apparently named by an admirer of the French emperor Napoleon Bonaparte, most likely a French explorer of the North West Company.

A few miles north of Cache Creek is the nicely restored 1860s Hat Creek Ranch Museum and Roadhouse, situated near the junction of the old Cariboo Wagon Road, today referred to as Highway 99. Midway between this historic site and Cache Creek is the St'uscwtews First Nation, formerly known as the Bonaparte Band. Near the side of the highway stands St. Louis Church, built in 1890 by two Russian carpenters commissioned by the widely known and revered Oblate missionary Father Jean-Marie-Raphaël Le Jeune.

Exterior renovations to the church began in 1990 and were blessed on April 14, 1991. Members of the Bonaparte Band participated in the restoration process.

The main structure of St. Louis Church is somewhat plain and unembellished, with the exception of the tall, square tower, which comprises a recessed front entryway and steeple. The top of the square tower has been meticulously embellished, with an appealing balustrade around its perimeter. Above the tower is a multi-louvered octagonal drum that supports a dome-shaped steeple, ball and cross. The dome is elaborately detailed with many gabled elements, creating an intriguing and satisfying appearance.

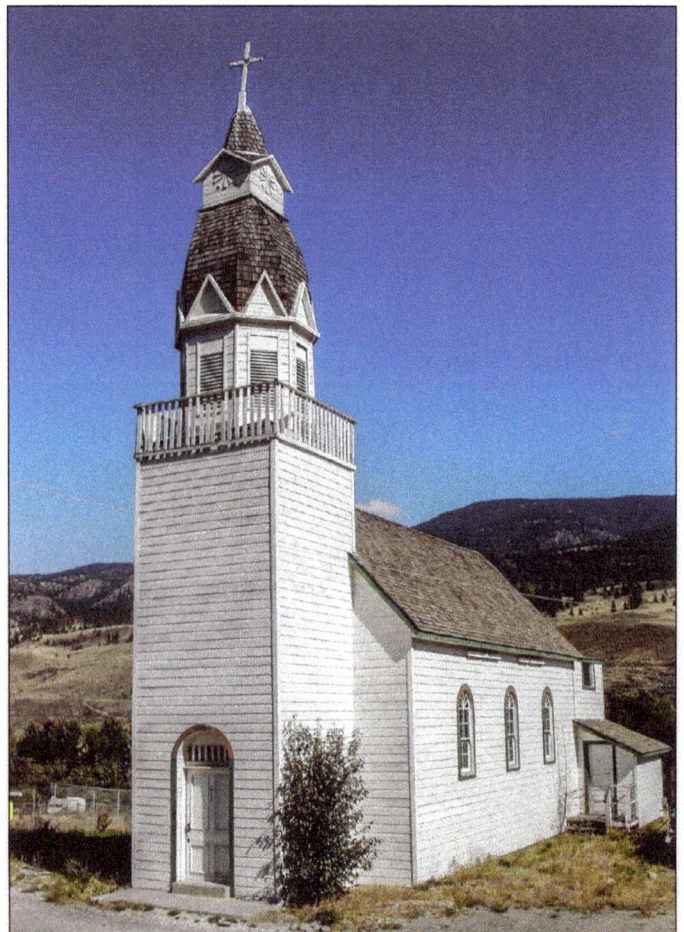

OUR LADY OF LOURDES
- 1983

Upper Nicola – Quilchena

Three miles north of Quilchena, at the junction of Highway 5A and the Douglas Lake Road, is the site of the first church in this area. The church, dedicated in 1893, was probably the third Catholic church in the valley. In 1901 Father Le Jeune described the church of Our Lady of Lourdes as a neat little building some 20 feet by 40 feet. A 600-pound bell was installed under the steeple, and a statue of Our Lady of Lourdes was placed on the altar. The bell, "Bernadette," as it was affectionately known, was donated by Mr. Joe Guichon, as well as other sponsors noted on the bell, including O'Rourke and Mrs. Josephine Guichon. The chief at the time was Celisten Shilhitsa.

Unfortunately, this fine old church burned down in 1979. The bell and statue survived the fire and are now enclosed in a shrine close by, dedicated to the Blessed Virgin Mary.

A new log church was constructed on the same site on the Quilchena Reserve and was blessed by Bishop Lawrence Sabatini on October 29, 1983. The new building is a unique structure; one of its outstanding features is the open bell tower that is centrally built into the main framework of the church. This extraordinary tower is completed by a four-sided, tapering bell-cast spire, which complements the overall project.

The exterior log corners of this attractive landmark were skillfully sculptured into a rather pronounced curve that accentuates its appearance, a one-of-a-kind edifice in the region.

ST. NICHOLAS'S CHURCH
- 1887

Spahomin – Douglas Lake

About a 90-minute drive south of Kamloops is the ranch of the famous Douglas Lake Cattle Company, long considered Canada's largest cattle "empire" at half a million acres. The ranch began in 1872 as a small homestead established by John Douglas in an area called Upper Nicola. Throughout this area, ancient aboriginal trails crossed the open range lands from Quilchena to the small settlement of Westwold, formerly called Grande Prairie. Over time, these trails evolved into wagon roads now referred to as the Douglas Lake Road.

Near Douglas Lake and the homestead is the aboriginal community of Spahomin, whose people have occupied this area for more than a hundred years and other parts of the region for thousands of years. The Spahomin area is now called Upper Nicola. Many generations of local First Nations people have been employed on the Douglas Ranch.

In the early fur trade period, what's now known as Upper Nicola was named for the revered chief Hwistesmexe'quen (Walking Grizzly Bear), who had been dubbed Nicholas by the fur traders. The traders recognized Hwistesmexe'quen as

the most powerful and influential chief in the southern Interior. The French pronunciation of his Christian name eventually was rendered as simply Nicola.

The first church at Spahomin was dedicated to St. Agnes in 1887, and Father Jean-Marie-Raphaël Le Jeune was involved in its construction. Later on, the church was renamed after St. Nicholas to honour the memory of the chief.

St. Nicholas's Church is very characteristic of early frontier construction methods: sturdy, unassuming but somewhat charming in its beautiful setting of grassland and rolling hills, rustic and in unspoiled condition.

St. Nichola's Church, 1969.
Photo from *Old Wooden Buildings*,
Hancock House, 1978

St. Nichola's Church February 2006

ST. PHILIP'S ANGLICAN CHURCH

Nooaitch – Lower Nicola

West of the south-central Interior town of Merritt, near an area called Canford, is the First Nation community of Nooaitch and a great stop of interest at the Spius Creek Hatchery, where Chinook and Coho salmon hatchlings are reared. The Nooaitch First Nation community was established in 1878.

Within the village stands the abandoned St. Philip's Anglican Church, which was built in the late 1800s or early 1900s. The general condition of this structure is very poor and seemingly destined to be pulled down within the next few years or brought down by the erosion process of Mother Nature, whichever comes first.

Architecturally, this church has little to distinguish it in the overall design; it is more or less a plain, unembellished building of its period. However, the bell tower does incorporate eight diamond-shaped openings in the belfry, a detail not often seen. In addition, the two windows on each side of the main building are nicely framed and offer a good example of frontier Anglican architecture.

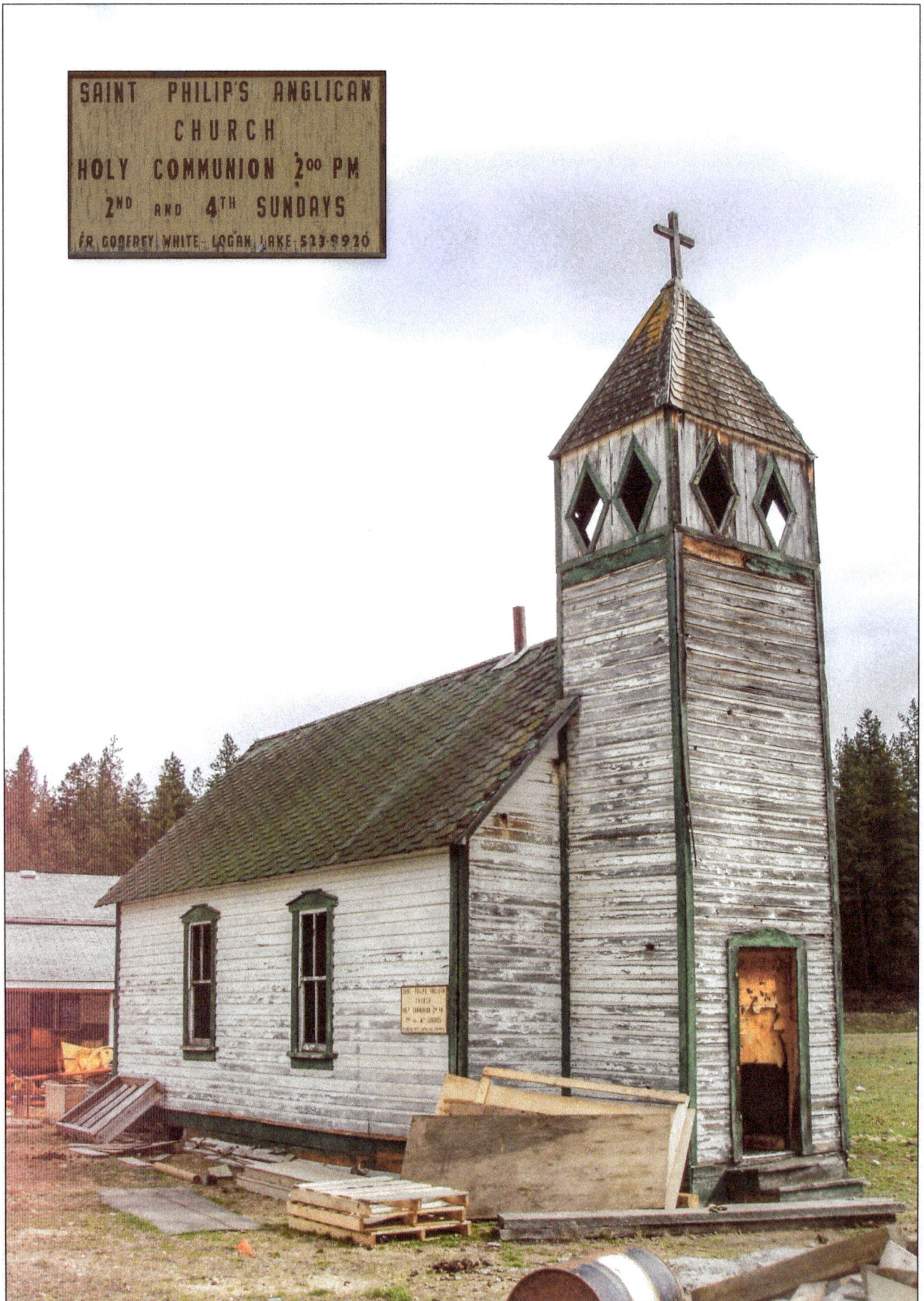

CHURCH OF THE
IMMACULATE CONCEPTION &
ALL SAINTS CHURCH

Shulus – Lower Nicola

A short drive west of the well-known crossroads city of Merritt on Highway 8 is a small, thriving community called Shulus, home to the Lower Nicola Band, which was established in 1878. According to some people there, the name Shulus means a large open space or area.

The area encompasses the Nicola River Valley and the outstanding Promontory Hills to the northwest. Promontory Mountain, once the location of a forestry lookout tower, is now a recreational viewing site. On a clear day one can see the city of Merritt and at times Mount Baker, across the border in Washington.

Within the village of Shulus are two old heritage churches, one Catholic and the other Anglican: the Church of the Immaculate Conception and All Saints Church, respectively.

The Church of the Immaculate Conception appears to have been built prior to or just after the turn of the last century. The side windows and front entrance doorway are in the gothic tradition, characteristic of most Catholic churches.

Notably, the drum is stylized by eight ogee-curved openings. This detail, combined with the four-sided bell-cast roof and its decorative cut shingles of various sizes and patterns, adds a rather pleasing element to the main structure of the building.

Located a few hundred yards away is the Anglican All Saints Church, which was probably built sometime in the early 1900s.

In contrast to the typical pointed-arch (gothic-style) windows, this church incorporates several tall, narrow side windows adorned with a top pediment, a signature mark of the Anglican tradition.

In addition, a respectable gabled porch roof over the front doorway adds to the overall design of the building. The roof is supported by two posts that are detailed with curved upper corner brackets. At the entrance to the property is a modestly constructed lych gate, a feature that is often seen outside Anglican churches of this period.

ST. PAUL'S CHURCH

Coldwater – Merritt

For the past 150 years, millions of people have traveled through the Coldwater River Valley along foot trails, roadways, a major highway and even a railway. Trappers, fur traders, gold-seekers, entrepreneurs and would-be cattle barons have all experienced the natural beauty and hardships of this major gateway valley to and from the coastal regions of the lower mainland.

One of the most interesting methods of transportation through this area is the renowned Kettle Valley Railway. It was constructed in the early 1900s and weaved through and around rugged, mountainous terrain and valleys between Midway and Merritt. It was a remarkable achievement of engineering by Andrew McCulloch. However, it was a relatively short-lived project; its operations were terminated in the late 1950s.

Twenty-six years later, a new multi-lane high-speed highway was opened between Hope and Kamloops, the Coquihalla Highway. The opening of this modern freeway coincided with British Columbia's Expo 86 world's fair and Vancouver's centennial.

More than a dozen kilometers south of Merritt on the Coldwater Road is the Coldwater Band (C'eletkwmx), established in 1878. Oblate Father Jean-Marie Lejacq visited the area in 1882, and in 1901 Father Le Jeune remarked that the people there had erected a pretty little church. The original church was named St. Paul's to honour the saint and give recognition to Paul Satchie, who was its main builder and a good example to his people. A newer church has since replaced the old structure, probably in the mid 1960s. It's a modern building, pleasing to the eye and modest by design, a house of worship situated in the picturesque Coldwater River Valley.

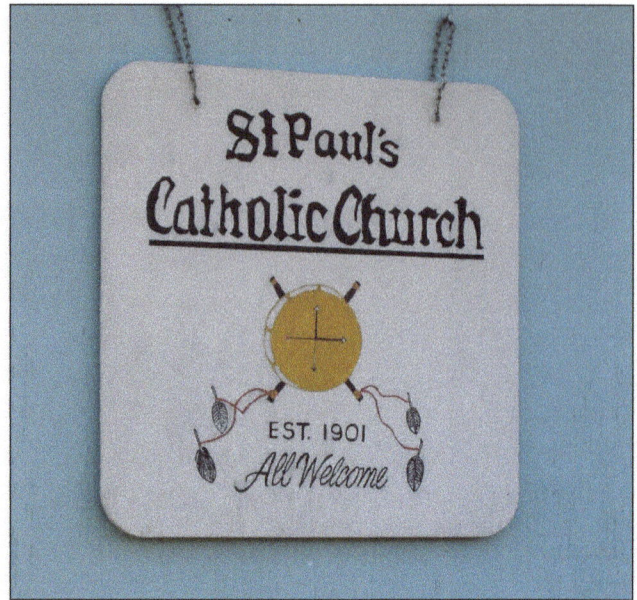

ST. CATHERINE'S ANGLICAN CHURCH

Shackan – Spences Bridge

The road from Spences Bridge to Merritt is often referred to as the Nicola River Highway. It's a secondary road that winds through a beautiful, semiarid valley with magnificent landscapes of sagebrush, pine, mountains and ranchlands. Points of interest, old buildings and defunct railway trestles can be seen throughout the valley. The old railway system was once commonly known as the Nicola, Kamloops and Similkameen Subdivision—NK&S.

This back-country road passes through several small communities, in particular the village of the Shackan Band, established in 1878. At the rear of the residential area, near the base of a large hill, is a very attractive rustic log building, St. Catherine's Church, built in the early 1900s.

This well-made log structure, with its carefully cut dovetail square corner joints is an exceptional execution of log construction design. The main side windows are typical of those used in other churches in the region. The roof is well built, with wooden shingles, and maintains the essential characteristics of log structures of the 1800s. This wonderfully preserved structure has survived extremely well over the past hundred years—certainly a testimony to excellent craftsmanship and design.

ST. JOHN AT THE LATIN GATE

- Ashcroft -

In 1862, Clement Francis and Henry Pennant Cornwall settled in the upper bench lands west of the pack trail above the Thompson River and southeast of Cache Creek, naming their place Ashcroft, after their family home in England. They built a grist mill and sawmill to supply products to new settlers in the area. The Cornwall Ranch soon became a thriving enterprise.

When news of a new road was coming their way, the Cornwall brothers quickly realized that a lucrative business opportunity could be had. The new road that was being built by the Royal Engineers would essentially allow hordes of gold-seekers, speculators and new settlers into the region. The Cornwalls promptly built a roadhouse and saloon on the south side of the new road, which they named The Public. The roadhouse served thousands of passing freight wagons and stagecoach operators throughout the 1800s and early 1900s, while at times also serving as a courthouse, jail and post office.

From the 1880s on, the famous roadhouse went by the name Ashcroft Manor, and remained a popular stop for weary travellers well into the automobile age.

Clement Cornwall became one of British Columba's first senators after Confederation with Canada in 1871, and Lieutenant-Governor of British Columbia in 1881.

Between 1880 and 1891, the Cornwalls built a small frontier log church on their ranch. At the turn of the last century, their church was moved to the Ashcroft Band reserve just south of the present Ashcroft Manor Teahouse.

The building style of St. John at the Latin Gate is an excellent example of square log construction, each log expertly assembled with tight dovetailed corner joints. The exterior arched windows at the side are modest and suited to its structure; the front door is framed with a flat board trim, with an uncomplicated pediment over the doorway.

The interior walls, vaulted ceiling, pews and altar are nicely treated with clear varnish that accents the woodgrain. The altar is an outstanding piece of carpentry, embellished with five arch-style panels that are set into an attractive colonnade-style frame structure. The center panel has an elaborately handcarved wooden cross element, which completes this impressive work of craftsmanship. St. John at the Latin Gate is an important part of the community and is still in use today.

St. John c. 196o's.
Photo from *Old Wooden Buildings*,
Hancock House, 1978

St. John, April 2019.

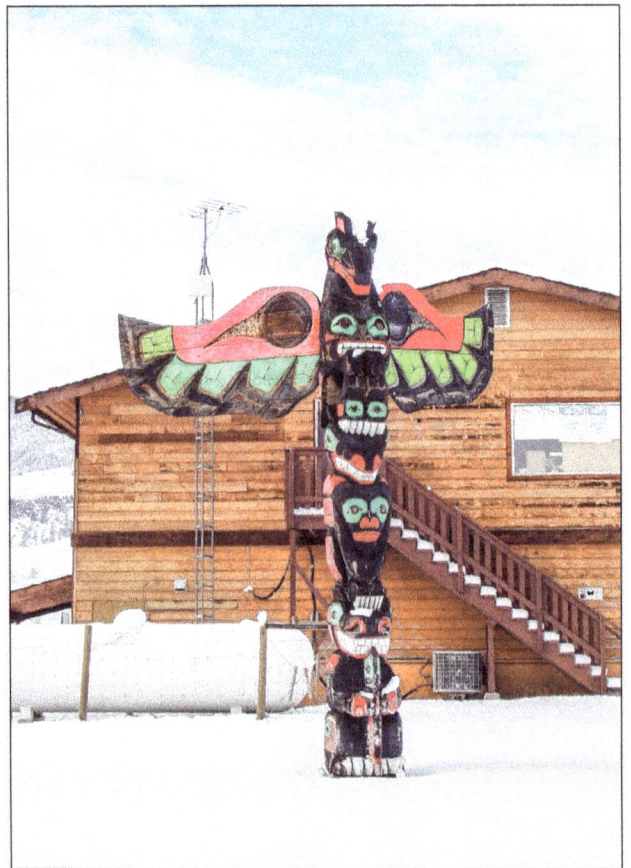

ST. AIDAN'S CHURCH

Pokhaist – Spences Bridge

Approximately 19 kilometres (12 miles) northeast of Spences Bridge on the east bank of the Thompson River stands an old, abandoned church at one time was known as St. Aidan's Church. The general terrain of the area is a mix of mountains and scattered tableland stretches of arable land. Sagebrush and cactus are common throughout the Thompson Valley. This location was called Pokhaist or Pukaist, depending upon which map one uses.

Evidently, about 80 to 100 years ago, there was a major rock slide close to an aboriginal village, which unfortunately forced most of the people there to move to safer ground. All that remains at the old community of Pokhaist is the abandoned church and a single dwelling close by that appears to be occupied.

The church structure, what's left of it, is a fine representation of early frontier construction: typical pointed-arch windows; a two-tier bell tower that unites the main entrance, and an unembellished belfry. The combination presents well in the surrounding landscape.

Amazingly, several interior furnishings have survived the decaying process, items such as the altar, pews and a small wooden candle remain intact. In addition, a wonderful hand-carved, high-back chair in good condition has also survived. The chair was presumably used by the visiting priest, a rare find in a vacant building in its present state.

St. Aidan's, June 2009.

St. Aidan's c. 1960's.
Photo from *Old Wooden Buildings*, Hancock House, 1978

ST. MICHAEL & ALL ANGELS
- 1905

- Spences Bridge -

St. Michael & All Angels Anglican Church is believed to be the second church in the history of this area. Local lore suggests there was a small aboriginal church belonging to the Church of England in the area prior to 1905.

This area was once known as Cook's Ferry, named after a man named Cook and his partner, Kimball. These men operated a barge-like ferry that was propelled across the Thompson River by pulling on a rope anchored to the river banks in the early to mid-1800s.

In 1864, a bridge was built across the river, essentially supplanting the ferry, thus ending a decade or more of service to the region. A similar ferry was in service during this time further upstream at Savona.

St. Michael & All Angels is plainly built, with its exterior walls, façade and bell tower covered in cedar shingles, excepting the main roof and front porch, which are covered in asphalt shingles.

The bell tower has four pointed window openings at the top, and it appears the original bell is still in place. The main side windows are rectangular and quite plain. It also appears there was at one time a transom window over the front door.

While it wears its age fairly well, one can see tie bars anchored beneath the eaves which suggest that there may have been structural issues recently. Beyond that, this church remains a landmark for the thousands of people who pass by each year.

This wonderful old church is at the southern entrance to the community of Spences Bridge.

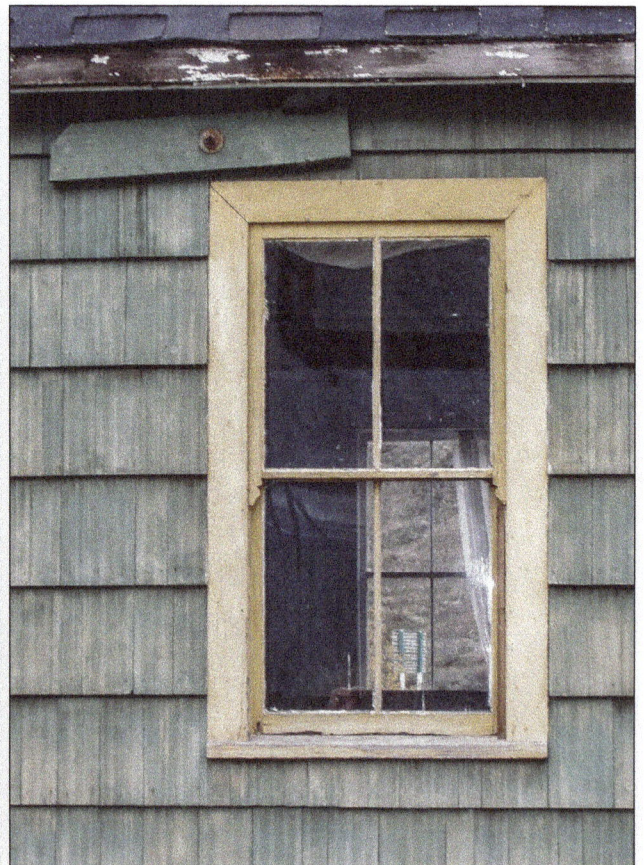

HOLY TRINITY CHURCH

Pavilion – Lillooet

Twenty-plus miles west of the historic 1860s Hat Creek Ranch & Road House on Highway 99, formerly known as the Old Cariboo Wagon Road, is the Pavilion, or Ts'kw'aylaxw (frosty ground) First Nation, established in 1861. Within the main settlement is an impressive heritage church that was built in the early 1900s. It is a fine example of local carpentry work of the highest order; one of the builders of Holy Trinity Church was Chief Francis Edwards. This wonderful old church was restored about 18 to 20 years ago.

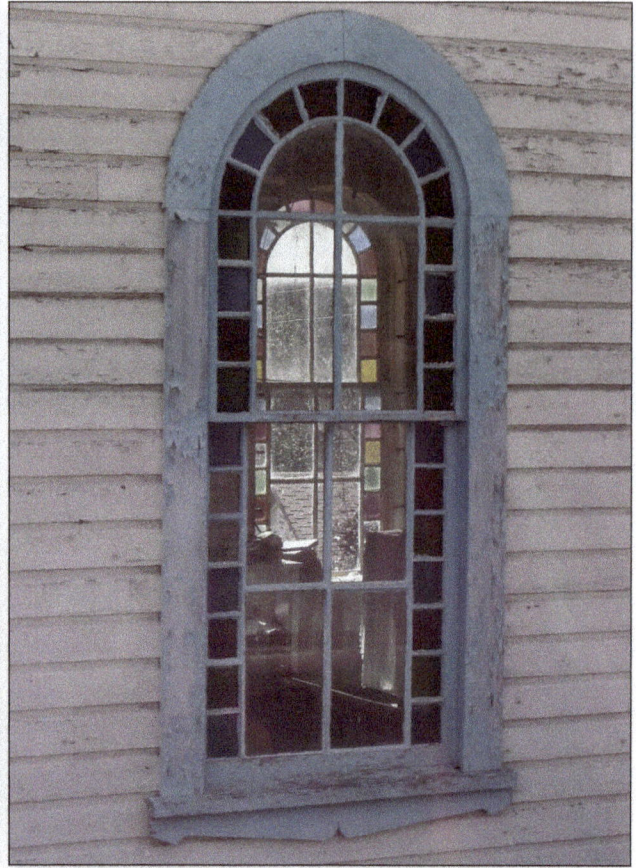

This classic structure has many architectural elements such as arched side window casings, scrolled bottom trim and stained-glass around the perimeter of the eight clear-glass panes. The façade has a tall, conventional bell tower topped off with an attractive open drum and an elaborately embellished rim around the bottom of the spire. The entrance door has been replaced by a modern paneled door that incorporates a small transom window. In addition, above the door frame is a larger transom window, as well as three arched windows similar to that of the main building.

OUR LADY OF LOURDES CHURCH

Fountain – Lillooet

High above the steep rugged canyon walls of the Fraser River, at a place called the great bend, is a large two-tier mountain plateau where the Fountain Band (now the Xaxli'p First Nation) settled in the later part of the 19th century. The community there is essentially split in half by the Cariboo Highway and the Fountain Valley Road. It's said that close to the junction of these two historic roads was an old assembly point where freight wagons and packers teamed up for the long journey to the gold fields in the north.

The origins of the name "Fountain" are uncertain, but it may have been bestowed by an employee of the Hudson's Bay Company when he came across a creek on a large flat area that ejected a stream of water similar to a fountain.

Directly northwest of this village are the beautiful mountains of the Camelsfoot Range, offering picturesque views in all directions. Roaming California bighorn sheep can be seen on occasion along the highway, a delightful wildlife experience for travellers passing through.

The upper tier of the plateau, just above the hayfields, has the main village and Our Lady of Lourdes Church. This relatively new church is the third building on this site since the turn of the last century. Its meager predecessor, from the 1950s, was an ordinary, squat-looking structure of simple design. During the 1990s this humble, inexpensive building was substantially renovated and expanded externally and internally.

This new church is a fine example of a rehabilitated 1950s building, with bright vinyl siding, modern arched windows and a grand set of concrete stairs that leads to the front doors. The bell tower is rather typical of church structures, except that this tower has been fitted with a tall, conical steeple.

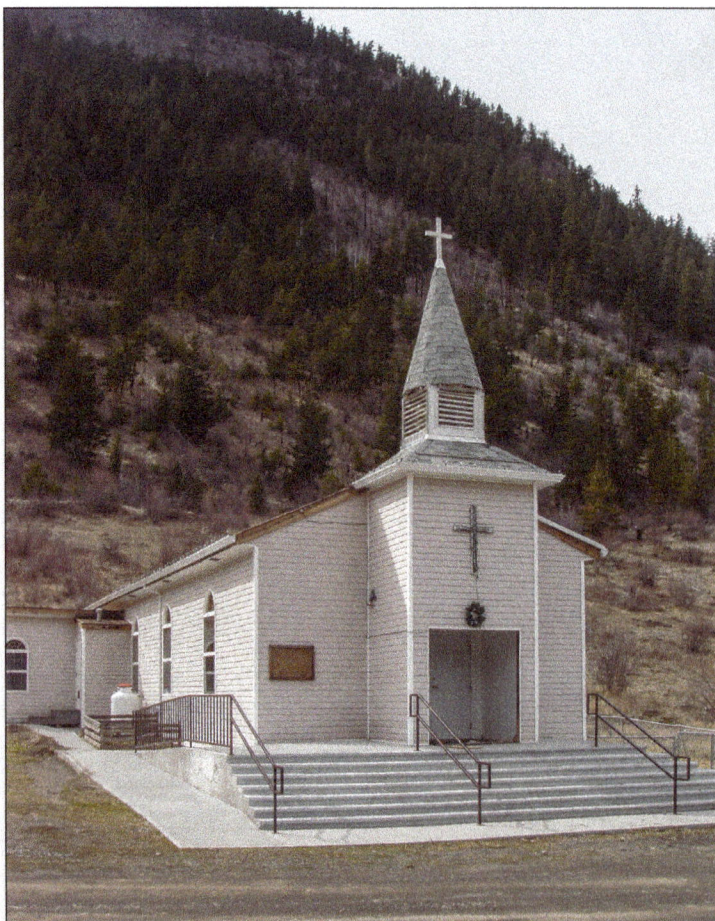

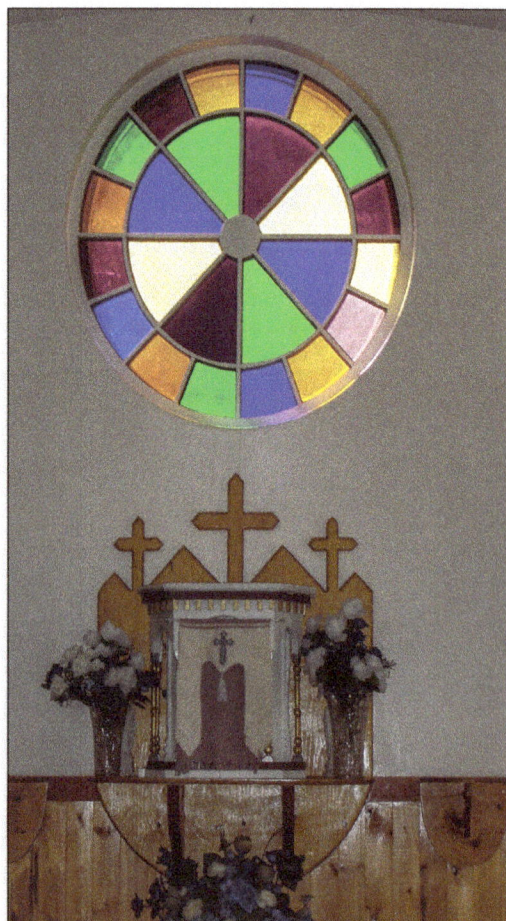

The interior reveals a wonderful combination of old and new components, such as many original statues, exquisite Stations of the Cross and pews that blend with the newer natural hardwood floors. Above the altar area is a round stained-glass window that emits a beautiful array of coloured light throughout the nave. Hanging from the ceiling are brilliant clear-glass chandeliers, and wainscoting embellishes the perimeter walls. An impressive setting to say the least.

ST. MARY'S CHURCH - 1916

- Enderby –

During the 1870s, Enderby became an important hub for the supply of goods and services as well as a transportation link for passengers during the navigable season. Stern-wheelers such as the SS Ethel Ross, SS Skuzzy and others regularly plied the rivers and lakes between Savona, Kamloops, Shuswap Lake, Sicamous, Mara Lake and up the Shuswap River to Enderby and back.

Enderby was regarded as the most northerly point of the Okanagan Valley and a direct overland supply link to the north end of Okanagan Lake.

By 1885, the main line of the Canadian Pacific Railway was completed and contributing to rapid growth in the Enderby region. Along with the growth came the need to transport finished products to markets far and wide. The railway station at Sicamous became the only viable option at that time.

In 1892 the Okanagan Railway began service up and down the Okanagan Valley, leading to the decline of stern-wheeler service to the area.

St. Mary's Catholic Church was established in 1894, but in 1916 was struck by lighting and burned to the ground. A new church

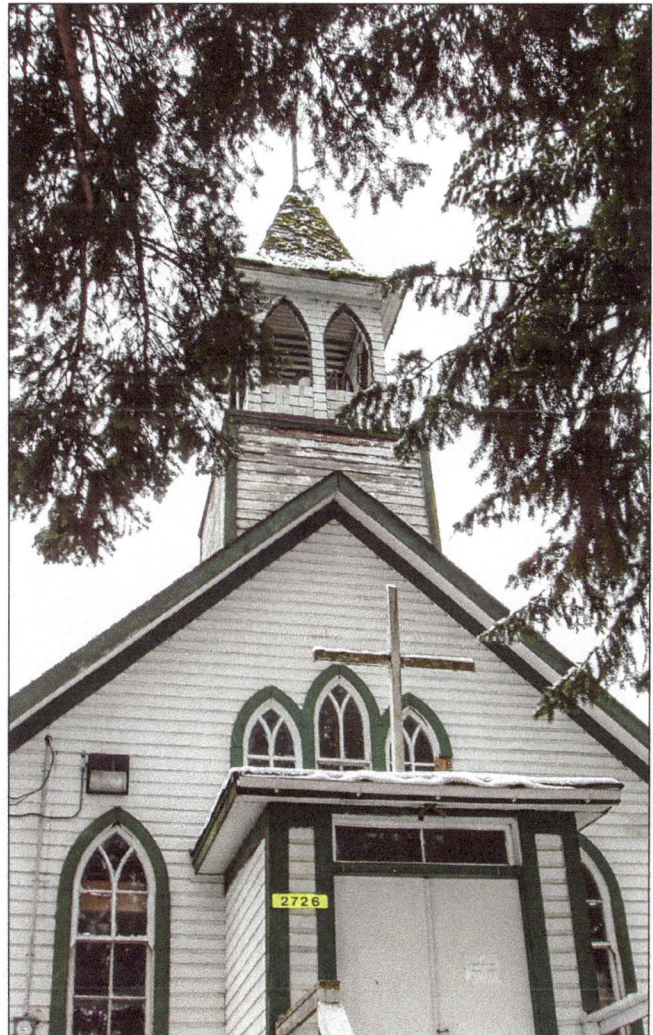

was immediately built, incorporating new elements. Triple gothic arched windows were installed above the covered porch, and a well-proportioned belfry on the roof. It was an impressive looking church, very attractive and graceful.

However, as the years went by, improvements inevitably became necessary. Recent restorations included a new metal roof for the main building as well as the bell-cast style roof on the belfry.

This church is a wonderful example of architectural design, solidly built and exceptional in every detail. It is indeed a tribute to those who participated in the restoration, a revered heritage church worthy of its parishioners.

St. Mary's in Enderby, 1963.
Photo from *Old Wooden Buildings*,
Hancock House, 1978

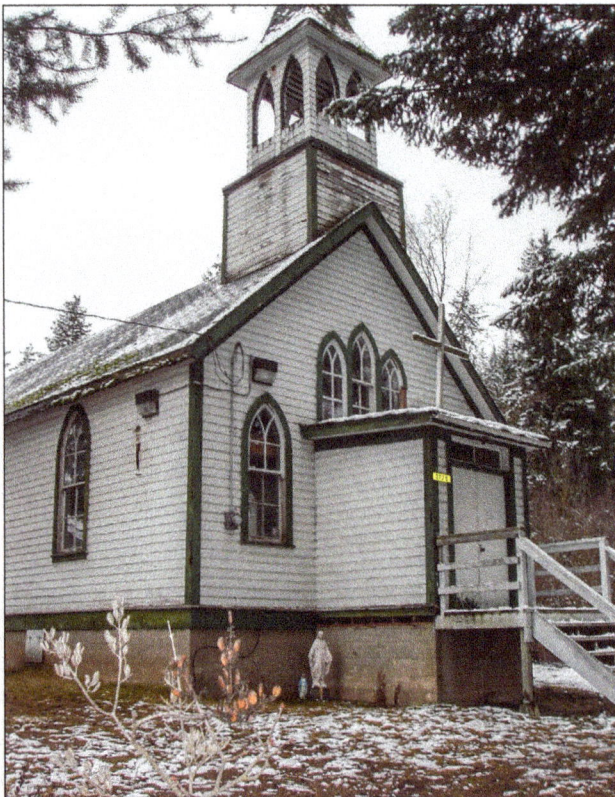

St. Mary's in Enderby, April 2019.

St. Mary's in Enderby, ca. 188-.
Photo from the Royal BC Museum Archives

ST. BENEDICT'S CHURCH

- North Okanagan Lake -

Close to the head of Okanagan Lake, near the junction of Highway 97 and Westside Road, is one of the earliest cattle empires in the Okanagan Valley. In 1867, Cornelius O'Keefe and partner Thomas Greenhow drove cattle from Oregon along the Hudson's Bay Company Brigade Trail, formerly an ancient aboriginal trail. A year later, O'Keefe homesteaded 162 acres, and within 40 years their cattle were grazing over 15,000 acres.

First contact between indigenous people of the area and white fur traders was made along the original indigenous trail on the west side of Okanagan Lake in the very early 1800s. First

Nations inhabitants of the region were, at that time, semi-nomadic. As fur trading activities increased, new settlers to the region also increased. In 1887, the Okanagan Band was forced to settle on the land set aside by the reserve system. These lands included the entire north arm of Okanagan Lake and the Salmon River Valley to the north.

The main community is about two miles (3.4 km) south of the old restored O'Keefe Ranch. Indigenous people of this community built a church there dedicated to St. Benedict at the head of the lake. It is, essentially, a conventional building with attractive round-arched stained-glass side windows as well as a wonderful matching Palladian-style window set above the front doors.

Fastened to the top of the gable-end roof is a squat, eight-posted open bell tower and cross. This church was probably built in the early 1950s.

ST. PATRICK'S CHURCH

- Westbank –

From early trails to modern highways: In this area, that transition began with the historic Okanagan Brigade Trail, which was developed from a network of aboriginal travel and trade routes that had existed for centuries. David Stuart, of the American Pacific Fur Company, was the first European to follow the trail from Fort Okanagan to Fort Kamloops in 1811. This trail was later used by the fur brigades of the North West Company and shortly thereafter by the Hudson's Bay Company.

Until the mid-19th century, fur traders passed by this area to exchange goods for furs with the Okanagan and Shuswap Nations and others further north. Traders, farmers and speculators soon settled along the west shore of Okanagan Lake. By 1902, the name Westbank was adopted for this area. The local reserve was named Westbank by the government post office to indicate its position on Okanagan Lake, and today the band goes by the name Westbank First Nation.

St. Patrick's Church is near the junction of the Old Okanagan Highway and Shannon Lake Road. The design of this church is quite basic and typical of the period. Side windows are in the gothic style; a modest but bold bell tower is deeply set into the main body of the church structure, essentially becoming the main focal point. Above the double entry doors is a plain single-transom window, flanked by matching pointed-arch windows.

The upper part of the tower combines a pair of louvered vent openings on all sides; the frame work around the

openings is nicely detailed and topped with a customary decorative pediment. The top of the tower culminates with a simple low-profile gable-end roof.

About three years after my first visit, the old church underwent a major restoration and expansion program. The general architecture of the old building remained intact throughout the entire project. This impressive new facility now combines church services with other multi-purpose uses.

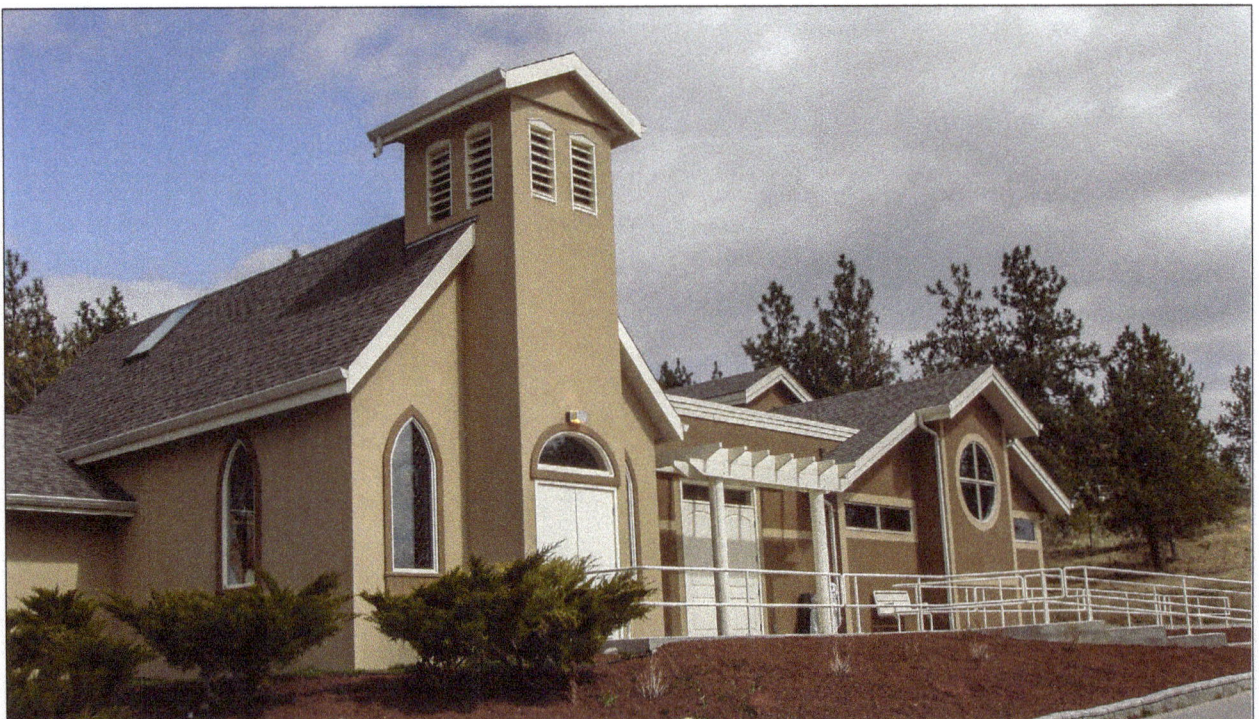

SACRED HEART MISSION

- Penticton –

Penticton comes from an Okanagan aboriginal word meaning the always place, presumably in the sense of a timeless place of occupation. Penticton was known as a major transportation centre in the early days. Paddle-wheelers carried freight and passengers to communities along the shores of Okanagan Lake as far as Okanagan Landing at Vernon, a distance of 80 miles (128.7 km).

However, this method of transportation came to an end when the Kettle Valley Railway appeared on the scene in about 1909-10. Shortly afterward, automobiles and freight trucks began to compete for a share of this lucrative market. These new methods of moving passengers and freight evolved rapidly, which altered and improved the way businesses were delivering their products to distant markets amid aggressive competition.

In spite of these changes, the old church on the Penticton Reserve has survived remarkably well throughout the years. This beautiful church now celebrates more than a hundred years of welcoming its parishioners. Sacred Heart Mission was constructed about the same time as the old Kettle Valley Railway.

Architecturally this church structure is impressive, charming and quite distinctive. It is well maintained—a credit to the people there. This solidly constructed building has a dramatic bell tower complete with a four-sided, bell-cast style steeple. The front entryway is adorned with a projected pediment supported by two flat columns that flank an attractive set of doors.

An impressive building, to say the least, pleasing to the eye and well suited to the area. This is a classic structure that was obviously built by skilled craftsmen.

ST. GREGORY CHURCH

- Inkaneep-Oliver –

In the southern reaches of British Columbia's Okanagan River Valley is the heartland of some world-class wine making. Vineyards dominate the region, yielding quality grapes fit for the best wines. Visitors enjoy panoramic views of a desert landscape that's home to rattlesnakes, sagebrush, many rare plants and invertebrates indigenous to the area.

Approximately midway between the towns of Osoyoos and Oliver, on the east side of the Okanagan River, is the site of Inkaneep and a Catholic mission by the name of St. Gregory. Inkaneep is part of the Osoyoos First Nation, which is surrounded for miles around by staggeringly impressive mountainous cliffs.

St. Gregory Church is a prominent building, located on the top of a hillside in the back country. Architecturally, it is a great example of local carpentry work, especially in the various window designs and in particular the large, three-tier sectional bell tower. The third tier of the tower is enhanced by a pair of ogee-style curved window openings on each side, adding a special touch to the overall composition of the main structure. The tower is completed with a low-profile pyramid roof and moderately embellished with a large white cross. St. Gregory is a very attractive church that was established nearly a hundred years ago.

ST. ANN'S

-Chuchuwayha -

After the discovery of gold in the late 1890s in the Similkameen River area, a wild stampede erupted throughout the region. In 1904, Hedley boomed with the opening of the mill town and the Nickel Plate Mine a short distance away.

From the heart of the Nickel Plate Mine, men took $47 million in gold. The nearby Headley Plate Mascot Mine, which was on a claim of less than an acre, mined a fortune. Finally, in 1955

the great body of gold, silver, and copper ore here was exhausted. The old buildings once used to process the precious metals remain standing high up the steep mountainside and are now a tourist attraction. This location is well known as "Famous for Gold."

Located between Stemwinder Mountain and Nickel Plate Mountain is the Chuchuwayha Reserve, home to the Upper Smelqmix First Nation, and St. Ann's Church. The church stands proudly on top of a barren knoll, like a sentinel overlooking the beautiful eastern Similkameen Valley below.

St. Ann's is a typical early frontier church, somewhat unembellished and conventional for its time. It is small, well preserved and very picturesque in appearance, with a mountainous backdrop. Outstanding features include arched side windows and louvered vents in the belfry. Simply, it is a delightful landmark for the hundreds of thousands of travelers who make their way each year over Highway 3, commonly referred to as the Crowsnest Highway.

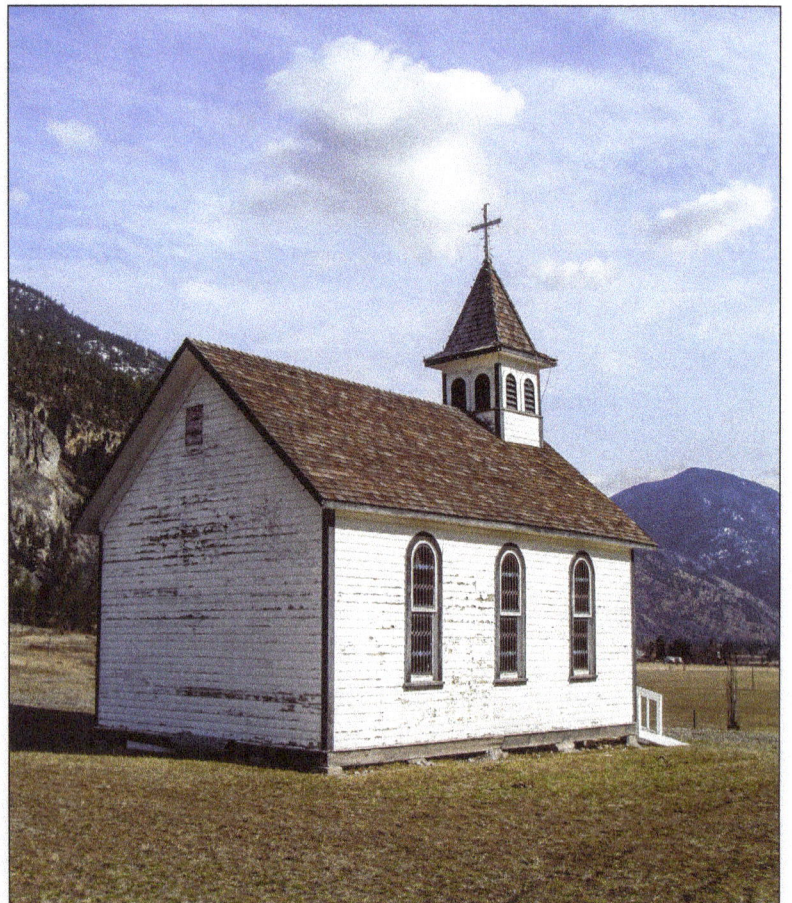

ST. THERESA'S CHURCH
- 1880s

Six Mile Creek – North Okanagan Lake

At a place just south of Highway 97 and the Westside Road junction is a small First Nations community referred to as Six Mile Creek. The Westside Road was then an important pack trail that passed by this community, regularly used by the great horse brigades of the Hudson's Bay Company out of Fort Kamloops. The brigades packed the much sought-after furs through the Okanagan Valley, terminating at the Columbia River, where the furs were loaded on barges and sent downriver to rendezvous with waiting ships at Fort Astoria on the Pacific Coast.

Father Jean-Marie-Raphaël Le Jeune was one of the first Oblates to minister in the Okanagan Valley, starting in about 1882. He travelled by horse and buggy throughout the territory from

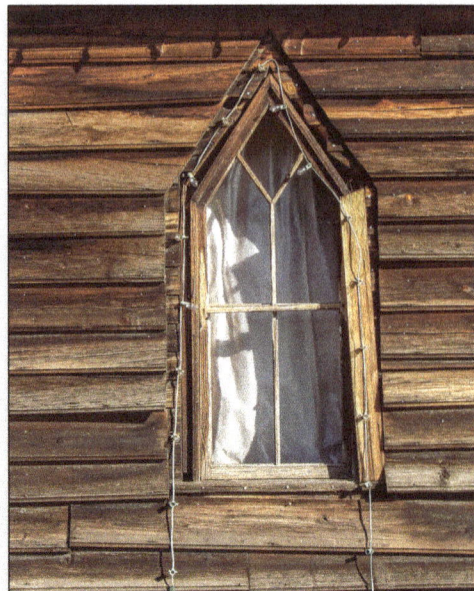

Fort Kamloops. During this period, a church was built at Six Mile Creek and dedicated to St. Theresa. The original construction was of rough-hewn logs, but at some later point the walls were updated with an application of clapboard siding, evidently to enhance its appearance.

The façade, while somewhat ordinary in composition, does show some elements worthy of mention. The front door incorporates two large windows and a small wooden panel beneath. Above the door is a triangular transom window imitating the rather sharply pointed side windows. There is evidence of what seems to be a square framed window in the gable, however, the glass is gone and the only remnant left is an exquisitely handmade wooden cross. This old building has held up remarkably well considering its age.

In 1966 it was decided that a new church should be built to replace the old structure, also dedicated to St. Theresa. The new building is a modern framed structure in the post-and-beam tradition. It is humble in appearance and functionally well suited for its time.

The front door is nicely embellished with three window elements aligned in the form of a cross. On top of the fairly flat gable roof is a small, flat-sided spire and cross. A few yards from it, in the front area of the church, is a tall, decorative cinder block column that supports a large bronze bell.

ST. ANDREW'S CHURCH
- 1870s

Cayoose Creek – Lillooet

Lillooet, formerly known as Cayoose Flats, is one of the oldest towns in British Columbia. It was widely recognized as a major centre of commerce for gold-seekers, jade miners and a variety of speculators who at one time or another passed through this thriving community.

During the gold rush period of the 1850s and 1860s, thousands of fortune-seekers converged at Lillooet, arriving via two main routes. One was a water and portage system that connected the Harrison, Anderson and Seton lakes. The other route was by a land trail through the Fraser Canyon to Lytton, then onward to Lillooet.

Packhorses, mules, and oxen were the principal freight carriers in the early years. At one time, Bactrian camels were also employed, however this venture turned out to be a colossal failure. These two-humped, awkward-looking beasts had a wretched disposition. They would spit, bite and become generally uncontrollable when in the company of other pack animals and their handlers.

The last straw, as it were, brought these great ships of the desert to an abrupt end. Sharp, jagged rocks literally lacerated their hooves, rendering them worthless as pack animals. Many of the camels were sold off as meat, some were let go to wilderness pastures, and several were taken to Westwold in 1864 for land clearing. One or two of these ornery brutes survived right up to about 1889.

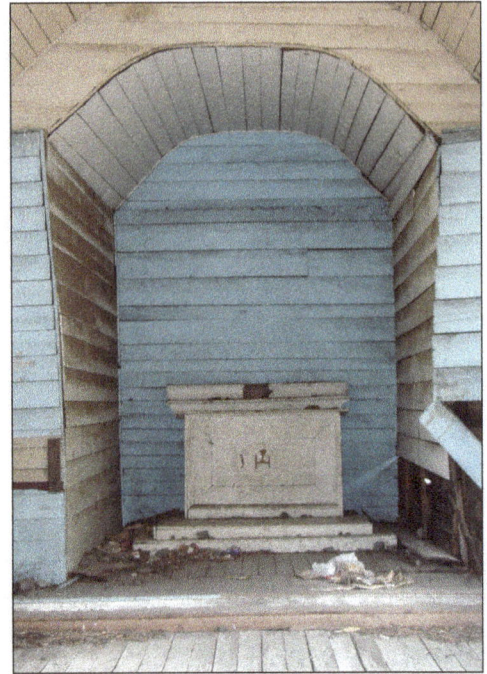

In 1981, a new highway bridge was opened for vehicle traffic across the Fraser River at Lillooet, uniquely named the Bridge of 23 Camels, the legacy of an ill-fated experiment—or, perhaps, simply a reminder of the boom-town era where the Cariboo Wagon Road began.

During the 1870s, a small frontier log church was built and dedicated as St. Andrew's Church, located a few yards off the old Seton Lake gold rush trail. The church has been abandoned for many decades; however, in the early days it was a distinguished frontier-style square log structure, complete with dovetailed corner joints and simple rectangular windows and front door.

The rooftop was originally adorned with a six-post open belfry and a short, octagonal dome. However, this somewhat attractive adornment withered away years ago, thus rendering the general appearance of this fine long-standing church as little more than a plain old cabin.

ST. AUGUSTINE ANGLICAN CHURCH

- *Nyshakup* -

High above the Fraser River along the Westside Road, midway between the towns of Lytton and Lillooet, is a small, semi-level patch of ground at a place known as Nyshakup, a First Nation Reserve. The general terrain of the area is typical canyon country: steep, rugged and prone to avalanche. On this site stands St. Augustine Anglican Church, which appears to have been abandoned for many decades.

The appearance of the church is rather meager and plain in style. The entire exterior is finished in wooden shingles, a practice uncommon in other parts of the country, where shingles were generally only used on rooftops and occasionally on parts of the façade as decorative elements.

Besides the obvious four-posted tower, which originates at ground level, the only outstanding features are the rounded-arch entranceway and cross above.

Sadly, this old building is beyond restoration and will likely disappear from the landscape in the very near future.

FAMILY CHAPEL
- 1978

- West Shore of Okanagan Lake -

This place of worship and meditation was built by the Swite family who were one of the pioneer native family's to settle here in the 1800's. They always believed that there was a better place to go when they left this earth; my father once said:

"When I wake in the morning, the sun shinning, breathing fresh air, birds singing, the sound of water trickling in the stream, everyone healthy, this is as close to heaven I want to be for now."
"Welcome to our place."

GARY F. SWITE

Undoubtedly, this humble eye-catching little Chapel is indeed a place of worship, as well as the smallest of its kind anywhere in the Province of British Columbia.

REGION – FOUR

KOOTENAY AND ROCKY MOUNTAINS

ST. PETER'S CHURCH

- Lower Kootenay -

In the picturesque valley of Creston is a place called Lower Kootenay. This valley, which the Kooetnay River runs through, boasts of breathtaking mountain views, lakes, streams and rich agricultural lands.

By the very early 20th century, farming and sawmilling had established a firm presence in the area. It was during this period that St. Peter's Church was built. This attractive little church stands today as it did when it was constructed, like a sentinel high up on the east bank near Creston, overlooking the Kootenay River.

This Catholic church is well proportioned, apparently largely due to Oblate Father Nicolas Coccola's understanding of church construction and architecture. The bell tower has three unique tiers. The open-arched bell tier supports a short, four-sided steeple. On the steeple are four nicely appointed gables that form a pleasing addition to the overall structure.

The windows are in the gothic style, as is the front entryway. The doors,

however, are not original to the church; they have been replaced with modern slab doors, typical of most churches of this age.

St. Peter's is a most delightful church and, for its age, is in good repair, certainly a testimony to the care and attention provided by the local inhabitants.

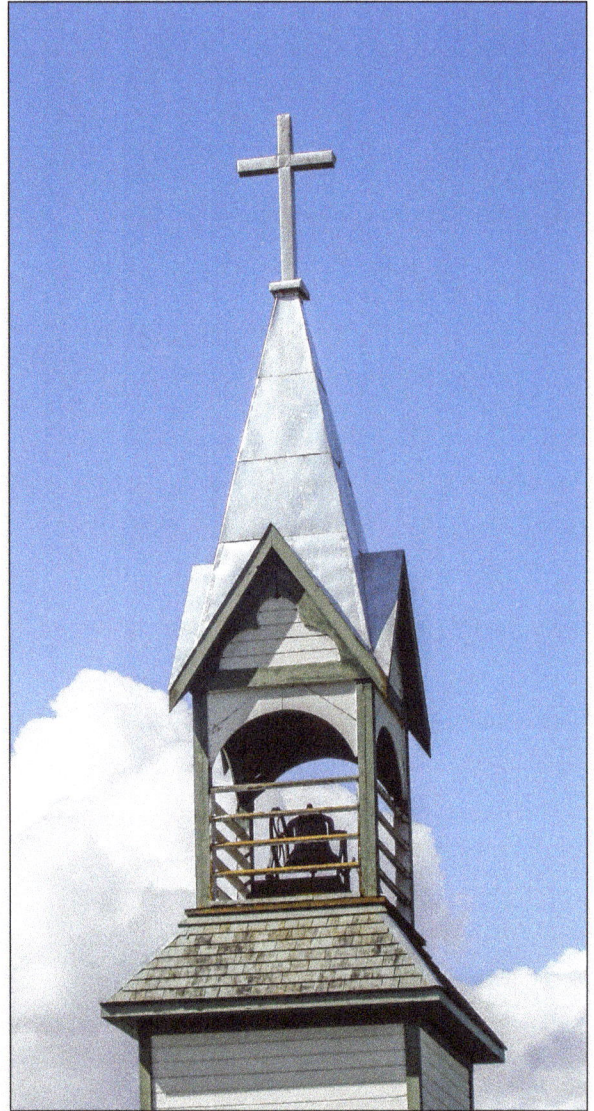

ST. PETER'S
- 1880s

- Invermere –

The recorded history of the Columbia Valley essentially begins with the entry in 1807 of David Thompson, explorer, surveyor, astronomer and fur trader of the North West Company. He was searching for the elusive great river that other Europeans, like Alexander Mackenzie and Simon Fraser before him, had failed to find.

Thompson built Kootenay House on Toby Creek where it entered a large river, soon to be named the Columbia River. David Thompson and his men paddled the Columbia, surveying its entire length, which emptied into the Pacific Ocean at a place called Fort Astoria. Not only did he map the great river; he also established fur trading forts and posts along the way. Thompson is accredited as the first surveyor in British Columbia.

St. Peter's Anglican Church was established in the 1880s near the Kootenay House site, at a place now called Invermere. It was a time when the valley was a hive of activity: agricultural pursuits, land settlement, and other industrial enterprises.

The main structure of the church is basic in design, as is the addition to the rear. The windows are rectangular and unembellished. However, the tower not only establishes this building as a church, it dominates the façade. The original doors are deeply recessed into the tower and nicely detailed with an arched framework.

At the bottom of the tower is an interesting decorative buttress-like element that has been applied to both sides. Near the top are plain louvered arches, and above that is a two-stage roof/steeple combination. The first stage is rather short and covered in fine, handmade scalloped shingles.

The steeple that forms the final stage is ornately bracketed, at least on two corners where the two components join; the other corner brackets appear to be missing. The steeple is also traditionally shingled and supports a ball to which an impressive decorative cross is mounted, a distinctive element that creates a dramatic effect on an otherwise humble structure.

SACRED HEART
- 1890's

- Columbia Lake – Windermere –

A short drive down the highway south from St. Peter's Anglican Church at Invermere is another church of similar design, Sacred Heart Catholic Church. The only elements that set this church apart from the one at Invermere are the pointed windows and a rectangular transom window over a single front door, which is noticeably offset, left of center.

The main building, tower and porch area have been fortified with a substantial concrete foundation. Overall, some further restoration is needed, such as paint and trim elements, including an upgrade to the cross on the steeple. Apart from that, this is an exceptional heritage church.

ST. EUGENE'S CHURCH
- 1897

- Cranbrook -

In the southeast corner of British Columbia flows a large, meandering river known as the Kootenay River, whose course passes by many communities such as Skookumchuck, Fort Steele and Wardner.

In 1865 and again in 1876, the area became a mining mecca, drawing thousands of men seeking gold and hoping to strike it rich. The most notable areas were Wild Horse and Perry Creek. Almost overnight, tents, makeshift cabins and other structures sprawled throughout the region, much the same as during the 1858 gold rush at Barkerville, east of Quesnel. These two significant gold rushes set off a human stampede, as it seemed gold was easy to find almost everywhere.

A few miles south of the confluence of Perry Creek and the St. Mary's River is a small community named St.Mary's Band Reserve, of which St. Eugene's Roman Catholic Church is a part.

The valley there offers outstanding panoramic views of the Rocky Mountains to the east, indisputably a magnificent backdrop for this highly regarded Victorian-style church—perhaps the most extraordinary piece of workmanship and design in the province.

The façade displays an abundance of intriguing detail unequalled in the East Kootenay region. The tower is deeply set into the church structure, uniting a myriad of components that complement the overall design. The beautifully constructed double doors are flanked by corner buttresses, topped with a combination of large finials and crosses.

Above the entrance doors is an elaborately detailed, arched gothic window and a niche-like component that blends appropriately with all the elements of the lower half of the tower. The square drum, while uncomplicated in design, has nicely scalloped, louvered elements fixed to the four corner posts, which are finely trimmed with moldings.

A tall, modified bell-cast style steeple is finished in small, overlapping, square-cut shingles and adorned with four dormer elements large and small at its base. The top of the steeple is finished off with a large turned finial base and cross assembly.

On both sides of the church are four lancet windows separated by five slender buttresses.

This richly embellished church dominates the local setting, and its beautiful architectural form overflows with graceful, thoughtfully applied elements.

REGION – FIVE

CARIBOO CHILCOTIN COAST

ST. KATERI TEKAKWITHA
- 1984

- Alexandria -

St. Kateri Tekakwitha is named for the first North American Indigenous woman to be canonized; known as Lily of the Mohawks, she was an early convert who died in Quebec in 1680 and was made a saint by Pope Benedict XVI in 2012. The church is located on the west bank of the Fraser River near the original site of Fort Alexandria. The fort began its fur-trade operations under the name of the North West Company, a Canadian enterprise from Quebec. In 1821, the Hudson's Bay Company amalgamated with the NWC under the HBC banner. The fort was named after Sir Alexander Mackenzie, who had explored the upper Fraser in 1793, a time that is considered "first contact" in this area.

By the 1860s, the fort was relocated to the east bank of the river to accommodate a more lucrative trade with miners heading north to the great gold fields of Barkerville.

Originally known as Blessed Kateri Tekakwitha, prior to the saint's canonization, the church was built in 1984 on the lands of the Alexandria Band to meet the needs of the local residence.

The architecture is of a modern wilderness style, rough but solidly built. It is well positioned in a prominent location overlooking the local community and directly across from St. Paul's Church on the east bank. The entrance structure steps down from the main building and supports a six-sided tower and cross.

The roof is covered in a heavy-gauge metal that will outlast the traditional cedar shingle product and provide better protection in the event of a forest fire.

The arched windows are rugged in design and complement the log-style construction. Overall, this wilderness Roman Catholic church is nicely integrated into its natural surroundings.

ST. PAUL'S CHURCH
- 1907

- Alexandria -

Along the east bank of Fraser River, at a place called Fort Alexandria, the Hudson's Bay Company established a fur trading fort and supply depot. The fort became a central collection point for furs from the north country and was the most northern starting point for the great horse brigades that transported hundreds of bales of fur overland to Fort Kamloops and beyond, to Fort Colvile on the Columbia River.

Today a cairn marks the location of the old fort at a pullout off Highway 97, just south of Quesnel.

Not far from the old fort location stands St. Paul's Roman Catholic Church, built around 1907, according to the caretaker in the area. The church stands alone by a large single pine tree in an open grassy field overlooking the Fraser River. This venerable wooden structure is in poor condition and badly needs foundation work as well as restoration to the exterior.

The pointed-arch window frames are impressively detailed, with the arched portion giving the appearance of being supported by columns on each side of the lower section—overall, a pleasing and well-executed design.

While the exterior of St. Paul's is fairly typical of church construction of its period, the bell tower is not. The tower leaves the impression of being an afterthought; to some degree it breaks the continuity of the overall church design. However, the tower by itself is elaborately constructed in four separate and distinct elements, perhaps built by a local craftsman from the community.

Sometime in the past 20 years or so, a makeshift shed roof was added, presumably to help protect the front door and porch area.

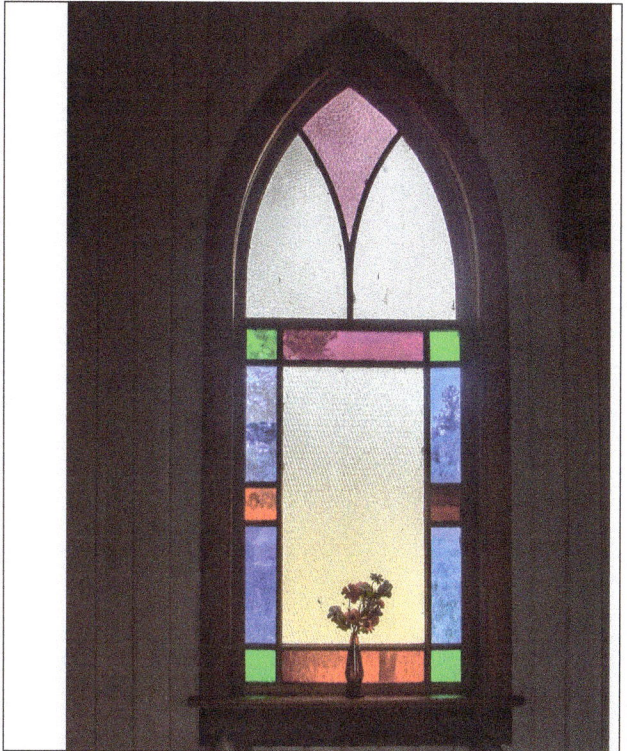

The interior of the church is, of course, entirely opposite to the rather windswept, wilderness appearance of the exterior. Upon entering the church, what you see is absolutely stunning. It immediately transports visitors to a place of calm. Its unspoiled condition is so welcoming, you might think you were either first to arrive or a little too late for a service.

The altar is a remarkable work of carpentry and original to the building. The statues flanking the altar are boxed with impressive sawtooth framing. The pews are plainly built but in exceptional condition. In the center of the room is an old wood-burning barrel stove for the comfort of the parishioners.

Decorative stained-glass windows provide a rich lighting effect that accentuates this setting of harmony, peace and worship. Decorating the upper areas of the walls are Stations of the Cross, and above them a distinctive lozenge and dentil cornice.

St. Paul's Church is occasionally used for weddings, baptisms, and other special occasions, a beautiful gem waiting to be rediscovered.

CHURCH OF
THE IMMACULATE CONCEPTION
- 1950s

- Dog Creek -

High up on the east bank of the Fraser River, overlooking the famous 1865 Gang Ranch to the west, is the small community of the Dog Creek Band. The main community is situated near the base of Dog Creek Dome, which rises to 3,280 feet.

The settlement here supports a growing infrastructure of commercial enterprises, housing development and employment opportunities. Dog Creek is also the site of the 1950s Church of the Immaculate Conception, which replaced an 1868 church by the same name.

The exterior walls of the building are finished in board-and-batten style and painted in a striking, deep sky-blue colour with white trim. The tower is eye-catching, with its wide base, single entrance door and transom window. Just below the main roof, the tower is set in and rises above the peak of the main roof, stepping in further to form the belfry. A simple design and well balanced to the overall structure.

The interior is very warm and inviting, with its high vaulted ceiling, handmade high-back pews and other decorative features.

ST. THERESA'S OF THE CHILD JESUS
- 1880s

- Alkali Lake –

About 15 miles (25 km) north on the Dog Creek Road from Dog Creek, a lush green valley opens up to an area where the Alkali Lake Ranch is located. The ranch is considered one of the oldest in British Columbia; it was established in the mid-1860s.

The Dog Creek Road was originally a trail that skirted the high ground above the Fraser River, used by many hundreds of gold-seekers making their way to the Barkerville region. This old route meanders through the present ranch in the same way it did almost 150 years ago.

A short distance from the ranch is the First Nations community of Alkali Lake, which offers most amenities required by its residents and travellers on their way through the area. Along

the main street stands the Church of St. Theresa of the Child Jesus. It is obvious a great deal of restoration work has taken place here. The church was built in the cruciform plan, with a large, square bell tower and front entryway.

The interior is in pristine condition, richly embellished with spectacular stained-glass windows, plus an extraordinary altar that dominates the sanctuary, along with many adornments and statues.

Above the entrance area of the structure is a beautiful vaulted ceiling over a balcony completed by an exceptional balustrade of rope-turned balusters.

This building is indeed a most impressive wilderness church, overlooking the picturesque valley of the Alkali Lake ranchlands.

ST. AUGUSTINE'S CHURCH
- 1991

- Canim Lake –

C anim Lake is one of the largest lakes in the Cariboo and is located about 35 km from the historic 100 Mile House, known as Bridge Creek during the Hudson's Bay Company fur-trading era.

In Chinook Jargon, Canim means canoe, which is appropriate since the Canim Lake First Nation settlement is close by. Canim Lake supports many fish species, especially the char, or laker as some prefer.

Notwithstanding the many private and community-operated businesses and other facilities on-site, there is one building that predominates against the community's mountain backdrop: St. Augustine's Church. This is a relatively new structure built from logs in 1986. It replaced the original 1897 church, which was destroyed by fire.

The new church is constructed in two segments, one larger than the other. Both elements have high, steep-pitched red metal roofs. To the right of the church is a four-posted open bell tower, supporting a new bell commissioned by the community. Adjacent to the church and bell tower is the cemetery, where handcrafted memorials mark the departed.

OUR LADY OF GOOD COUNSEL

- Soda Creek –

In the high plateaus and valleys of the central Cariboo, there are diverse landscapes: snow-capped mountains, clear streams, rivers, lakes, rich green forests and high, grassy rangelands, each contributing to a complex ecosystem intertwined with the fascinating frontier lore of a land called the Cariboo.

Among the hundreds if not thousands of tributaries of the Fraser River is one called Soda Creek, the name of which refers to its bed of natural lime, where the water bubbles like carbonated soda water.

During the 1860s, a fledging frontier town sprang up almost overnight amid the greatest gold rush in the history of British Columbia. Hotels, saloons, stores and other businesses were quickly established to meet the needs of a wave of thousands of enthusiastic gold-seekers.

For a short period, Soda Creek was the end of the Cariboo Wagon Road and the embarkation point where newcomers heading north boarded paddle-wheelers to be taken up the turbulent waters of the mighty Fraser River to various ports such as Quesnel Mouth (Quesnel) and Fort George (Prince George). As many as nine flat-bottom river vessels became the main transporters serving communities along a 400-mile (600 km) river route to the far north.

Close to the boomtown site of Soda Creek is the community of Xats´ul First Nation. It includes Our Lady of Good Counsel, a small Catholic church.

The church stands high up on benchland overlooking the Fraser River. The structure is quite basic in design; it has a plain barn-style set of doors flanked by tall narrow windows on the front. The side windows are uniquely built in three rectangular sections, combining two windows like the ones in the front and a taller version placed in the middle.

The bell tower is rather large and somewhat imposing, slightly out of balance with respect to the main church structure. The exterior is very clean, inviting and nicely paneled. The pews, while plain, are carefully varnished to expose the natural beauty of the wood grain.

Most of the community, which once lived close to the edge of the river bank, had to abandon their homes many years ago and relocate to higher ground. According to some of the local residents, the shore has suffered a lot of erosion; hopefully this problem can be rectified.

CHURCH OF
THE IMMACULATE CONCEPTION
- 1895

- Sugar Cane – Williams Lake –

At the northwest end of a large lake, ancient aboriginal trails from all directions intersected at a village called Columneetza, which is loosely translated as meeting place of important people, sometimes rendered as princely people or lordly people, depending on whom you ask.

This is where a fledgling frontier settlement by Europeans called Williams Lake was established. Today Williams Lake is considered a thriving supply hub for the Cariboo Region.

It is believed this large lake was named after a chief dubbed William by the colonizers, a notable and well respected person of the area. Others believe it was named for William Pinchbeck, an early settler, rancher, entrepreneur and peace officer. Certainly that's a question waiting to be resolved.

In 1881 a T'exelcemc First Nation reserve was established at a large meadow to the southeast end of Williams Lake, evidently named Sugar Cane because of the tall sweetgrass there, which was sought after by their horses. A sign at the entrance to this community reads "Welcome to Sugar Cane—Williams Lake Band."

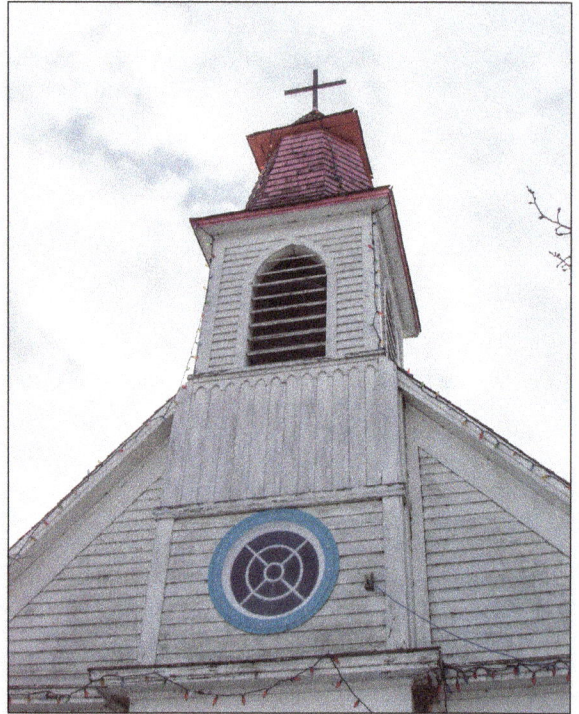

This is also the location of the Church of the Immaculate Conception, an impressive old church that includes many distinctive architectural elements. The structure has a rectangular floor plan, returned eaves and a unique bell tower flanked by two gothic-style windows.

The tower is deeply set into the main structure. The entrance has a series of overlapping cutout arched boards, each diminishing in size to form a deep, tapering entryway to a single door.

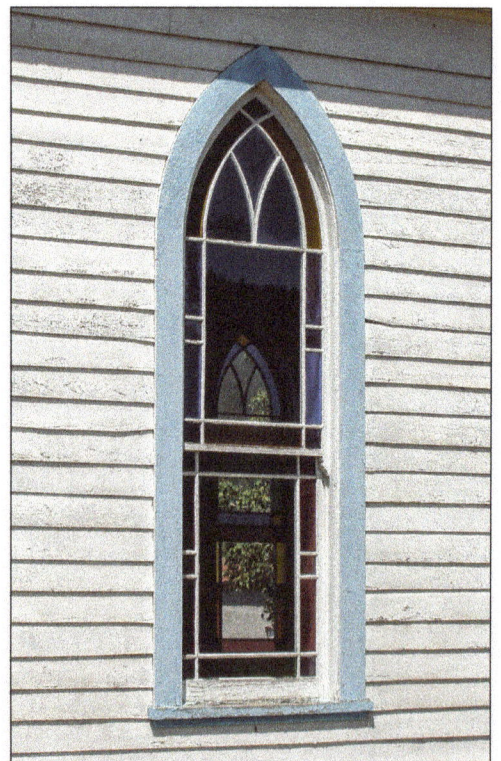

Above the door is an arched window. The gable area of the tower has a nicely placed bull's-eye window that lets the morning light shine through into the nave and sanctuary area.

The belfry is trimmed with several louvered boards mounted into an arched frame.

Further above that is what seems to be a two-part, tapering octagonal roof, one part stacked upon the other and culminating in a point where a sizable cross is mounted.

The rear of the church, while very plain, also has a bull's-eye window. Overall, this structure is a fine example of local carpentry work and a commendable effort at restoration by the members of its community.

ST. JOHN THE BAPTIST
- 1904

Stone – Hanceville

From the Fraser River in the east to the beautiful coastal mountains of the far west lies the magnificent Chilcotin Valley, a place of varied natural landscapes from grassy plateaus and meadows in high mountain ranges to deep canyon benchlands, all supporting a ranching lifestyle for more than a century. A true wilderness frontier stronghold that has essentially remained unchanged.

Just south of Hanceville, also known as Lee's Corner, is the Chilco Ranch; it was, at one time, the largest cattle ranch in the Chilcotin Valley. Its humble beginnings date to the late 1800s, from which it grew to almost a million acres of deeded land.

Many First Nations people worked on the Chilco Ranch over the years. Adjacent to the ranch is the small Stone Reserve, home to the Yunesit'in First Nation, whose current economic activities include cattle ranching, agriculture and forestry. Within this community stands a lovely early church called St. John the Baptist.

The church was built in 1904 by George Myers. It appears to be of frame construction and has undergone several renovations, each time making it better, according to Philip Myers, a

resident of Stone. Possibly the only thing that detracts from this pleasing old church is the rather unrefined shed-like roof over the front entranceway. Otherwise, it retains its pleasing architectural features. St. John the Baptist Church will continue to represent an interesting part of early church history in the Chilcotin.

SACRED HEART OF JESUS

Anaham

Along Highway 20 a few miles east of Alexis Creek in the Cariboo Chilcotin region, is the community of the Anaham (Tl'etinqox) First Nation. Nearby, numerous battles were fought against the Chilcotin people by marauding coastal tribes long before the arrival of the Europeans in 1793. According to oral history, they were fought at a place called Bull Canyon, also known as Battle Mountain. Warriors from all parts of the Chilcotin Territory gathered to fight against the invaders.

The endless drive of the indigenous people of this area to protect a land they called their own is a testament to their resolve when called upon. Likewise, their resolve to restore or rebuild a new church in the face of adversity bodes well for their community.

The first church here was constructed of logs in 1870. In 1923, it was replaced by a frame structure that served the area well until it began to disintegrate. To keep the building from literally falling apart, taut cables were stretched from wall to wall and buttresses added to support the overall structure.

Chief Maxine Mack and the Band Council finally declared that it was time for a new building. In 1979, a new church was built. But 27 years later, on January 6, 2007, that beautiful building was destroyed by an electrical fire.

Once again the people of this First Nation were determined to replace their beloved church, and a new log structure was raised in 2008 by Pioneer Log Homes of Williams Lake. This church is anything but an ordinary building; in fact, it's an extraordinary work of architectural design and workmanship.

This structure has three main components. The first is a 50-foot-tall log bell tower that supports a well-built, bell-cast style roof, with a large bronze bell beneath it, certainly a prominent feature of this facade. The other two components are also of log construction, detailed nicely with a large, multi-paned arched window mounted above the main entrance. The lower perimeter of the building is modestly adorned with a series of small, conventional, rectangular windows.

Overall, this church is a very attractive landmark and a wonderful expression of 1800s construction methods with the flair of quality modern craftsmanship.

VISITATION OF THE BLESSED VIRGIN MARY CHURCH

Anahim Lake

The Anahim Lake community is considered the gateway to the west coast and the world-renowned Tweedsmuir Provincial Park. Evidence of the famous ancient Nuxalk-Carrier Grease Trail, also known as the Alexander Mackenzie 1793 overland route, can be seen in the park. Indigenous people in the Interior guided Mackenzie over their familiar trade route to Bella Coola, the place where Mackenzie inscribed on a prominent rockface the words "Alex MacKenzie from Canada by land 22nd July 1793".

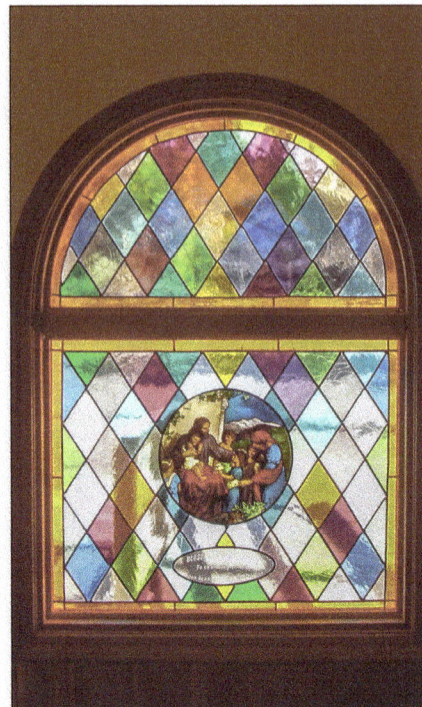

The region showcases abundant wildlife, world-class fishing lakes, and rivers winding through vast mountain ranges and valleys. It's a land that had supported First Nations peoples for thousands of years and was untouched by European fur traders and colonial settlers until the late 1700s, a period called "first contact."

Within the Anahim Lake community is the Squinas reserve of the Ulkatcho First Nation and the Church of the Visitation of the Blessed Virgin Mary. Entering the residential community, you are greeted with an attractive and rather outstanding church building, large and uncomplicated in design. Wooden lattice panels used on the front porch and bell tower complement the overall composition of the structure.

The interior of this fine church features a spacious nave, humbly furnished with naturally treated wooden pews and post-and-beam elements that accentuate its pleasing appearance. Flanking the nave area is a series of richly embellished, modern stained-glass windows that bring all the elements of the space into harmony.

CATHOLIC CHURCH
- 1892

- Nazko -

Nazko is a small rural community in the Nazko Valley, about 90 kilometers west of Quesnel. The area here is also known as one of the entranceways to the famous Nuxalk-Carrier Grease–Alexander MacKenzie Trail, a route had been used by First Nations people to transport trade goods such as oolichan oil and other food products to the Interior from the coast for centuries.

In 1793 aboriginal people guided fur trader and explorer Alexander MacKenzie and his men through Nazko country and beyond over this well-known trail to the coastal village of Bella Coola.

The Nazko Valley was also homestead country during the early 1900s. In more recent times, cattle ranching, logging and other community enterprises evolved to the country lifestyle we see today.

In 1892, a church was built in the village of Nazko by local residents under the direction of the Roman Catholic clergy. This church ceased operating in 1988, and now, more than two decades later, this once-fine structure has succumbed to the elements. It is believed that it will be dismantled to make way for a new building in the near future.

Architecturally this church is, in many ways, a basic frontier-style rectangular structure. At some point an addition was added to the rear of the building. Smaller gothic-style windows were incorporated, thereby creating a slight imbalance between the original building and the new addition.

Another interesting detail in the original building is that that the foundation was made of large-diameter logs positioned horizontally around the perimeter of the structure, giving it a strong base, or sill, a not unusual technique in its day.

However, at the lower left front corner, one can see that the log base had been notched out to receive the vertical wall studs. Also unusual was the use of round rafters in the ceiling rather than squared off rafters, as was customary in that period.

In the foreground and slightly to the right of the church, an octagonal gazebo-style structure now houses the original church bell, presumably removed from the bell tower due to the deteriorating supporting structure.

ST. THOMAS
THE APOSTLE CHURCH

- *Toosey – Riske Creek* –

A few miles south of Riske Creek, the gateway to Chilcotin Country, is the Toosey (Tl'esqox) First Nation. It is situated in an area of high grassland plateaus and rolling hills. Steep ravines and hoodoos border the western slopes of the Fraser River and the southwestern benchlands of the Chilcotin River. It is also a land of agriculture, logging, ranching and the California bighorn sheep.

Within its community stands St. Thomas the Apostle Church, a rather charming structure, well built and unembellished. The main building is house-like in style, with four rectangular windows on each side.

Attached to the front of the church is a nicely detailed tower incorporating two plain solid-slab doors; above the doors is a small spoke-wheel window. The belfry has a pleasant appeal with its double louvered openings and a unique four-gabled roof of equal proportion.

This church is active and is visited by the clergy on a regular basis.

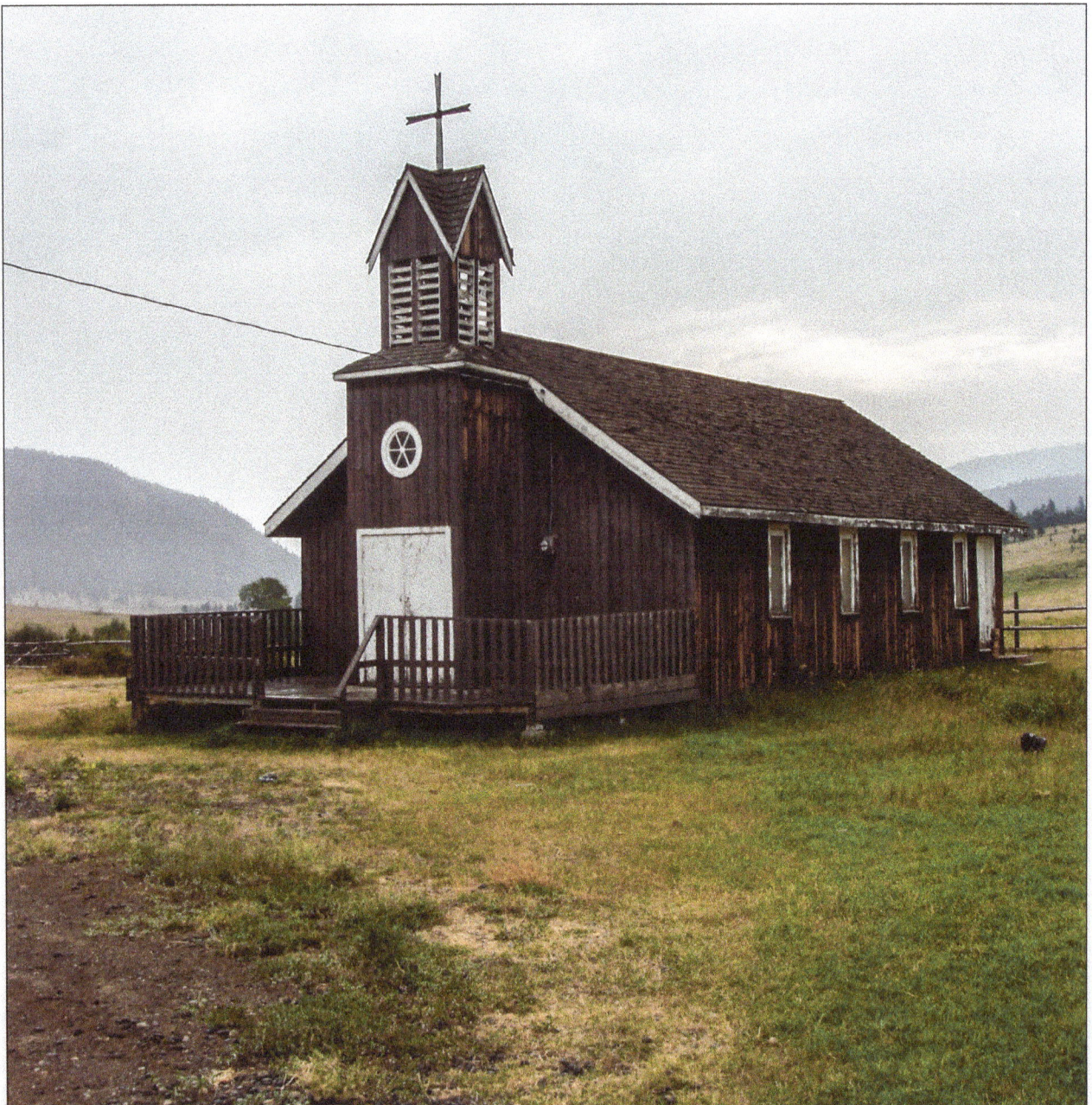

ST. PETER'S CHURCH

- Red Bluff - Quesnel -

During the great inland gold stampede of the early 1860s, Quesnel Mouth (Quesnel) was the jumping-off point for miners and speculators heading for the gold fields of Barkerville. Paddle-wheelers from Soda Creek plied the turbulent waters of the Fraser River to Quesnel, carrying thousands of passengers with high hopes of settling the land or finding their fortune.

The city of Quesnel was named after Jules Maurice Quesnel, who travelled with the honoured explorer and fur trader Simon Fraser in the early years of discovery and exploration of the Fraser River.

A few miles south from Quesnel's city centre is an area called Red Bluff, apparently given its name by the gold-seekers who worked the gravel bars of the Fraser River. On a bluff high above them on the east side of the river, the land appeared to be red, and from that time forward the area became known as Red Bluff.

A short distance from the reddish escarpment is an abandoned church that was built in the early1900s and served the Red Bluff community for at least 50 years.

St. Peter's Church, now commonly referred to by local residents as Red Bluff Church, stands in ruin, no more than an empty shell after vandalism took over a once admirable frontier structure.

The building was constructed with square-hewn logs that were expertly interlocked at the corners in the tight-fitting dovetail fashion. It was a method commonly used in the early 19th century by the HBC fur traders trading in a land they often referred to as New Caledonia, now called British Columbia.

Over many decades, the main structure underwent at least two major exterior changes. At some point the logs were covered over with cove siding, which is evident in exposed fire damage. The windows were built in the gothic style with nicely curved arched casings, as well as a curved arch in a rectangular louvered opening in the bell tower.

Years later, if not a decade or two, the exterior was once again enhanced, this time with newer, slightly wider, bevel siding that was applied over the existing siding. The windows remained in the gothic style, however, this time they were constructed in straight angular lines, forming an arch as seen here. The stained-glass windows were stylized in an aboriginal motif of brilliant blue, red, yellow, and green pieces of glass artfully crafted and assembled, a superb composition.

Unfortunately, only one window has survived, and this wonderful gem is the last piece of architectural beauty here; it is at risk and will probably not survive much longer.

The structure of St. Peter's Church is a typical wooden building of its period, modest in design and fitting for its intended use. Despite valiant restoration efforts by the community, this old church now stands as a reminder of a time that once was, rising alone in an open hayfield, left to the unrestrained elements of nature.

REGION – SIX

NORTHERN

OUR LADY OF GOOD HOPE
- 1873

Nak´azdli – Fort St. James

Located at the east end of Stewart Lake is the community of Nak´azdli First Nation (formerly Necoslie), which has occupied the area for many centuries. At one time prior to first contact there was a great battle at the mouth of the river between native groups from the south in an effort to protect their traditional territory. Nak'azdli, their preferred name since 1989, means when arrows were flying.

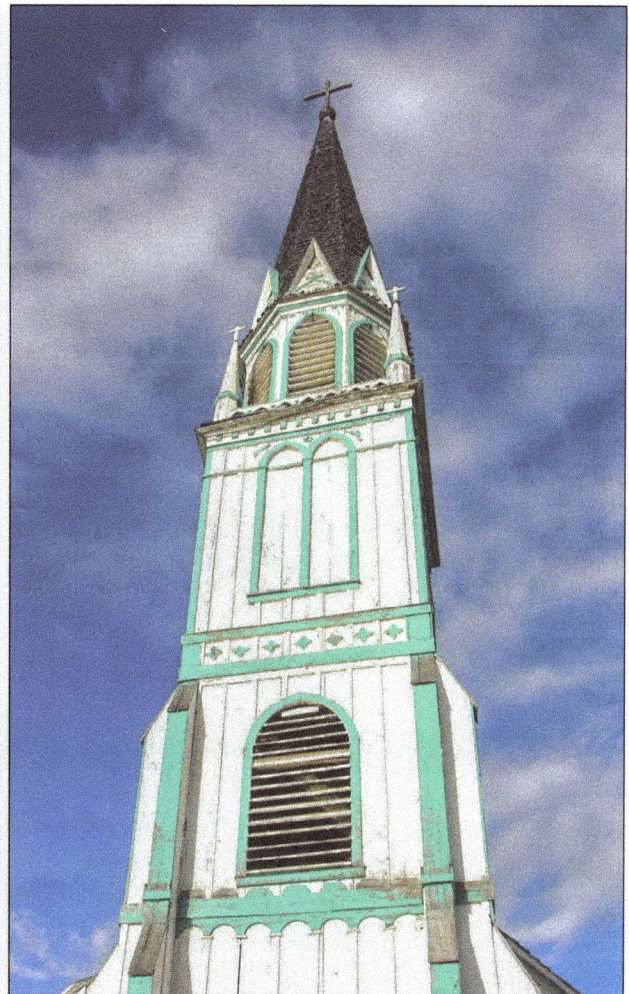

These people were extremely diligent in preserving their land base, which included the high ground called Nak'al, a high peak used as a lookout against possible hostile parties coming down the lake from the northwest. The name of this peak was later changed to Mount Pope, after a surveyor that worked for the Collins Telegraph Line in the late 1800s; it's now part of Mount Pope Provincial Park.

The First Nations people became an integral part of the fur trade with the North West Company, which had established a post in 1806 adjacent to them called the Stewart Lake Post. Its founder was Simon Fraser. By 1821 the Hudson's Bay Company acquired the post, which was shortly after renamed Fort St. James to honour Chief Factor James Douglas. The fort is now a fully restored National Historic Site.

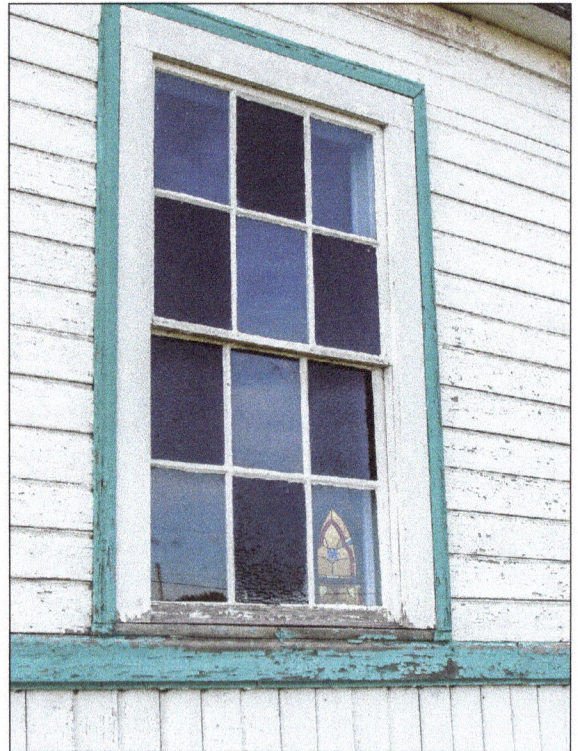

Over 60 years since the founding of Stewart Lake Post, Our Lady of Good Hope was built. It was originally constructed of square logs, with square windows and a plain bell tower. In 1905, Father Nicolas Coccola and the aboriginal people remodeled the church to look much as it does today. Every surface of the bell tower is covered with intricately carved woodwork. The drum has pointed-arch louvered openings and tall pinnacles at each corner, representing a high level of classic design and craftsmanship of the period.

HOLY CROSS CHURCH

Binche

Twenty-eight kilometers west of Fort St. James, along the north side of Stewart Lake, is the village of Binche, one of three communities under the governance of the Tl'azt'en Nation based at Tachi, 24 km west.

Binche village at one time was the main fishing site where the Tl'azt'en forefathers set up special containment weirs to catch salmon at the outflow of Binche Creek. The villagers were also highly involved in the fur trade—essentially forming the backbone of the trade during the years the North West Company headquartered at Fort St. James.

Between Binche Bay and Fort St. James, one can visit at least 21 heritage pictograph sites. Another attraction at Binche is one of the oldest churches in the province. This church, by the name of Holy Cross, is said to predate Our Lady of Good Hope at Necoslie (Fort St. James).

Holy Cross was apparently built near the shoreline, however after repeated flooding it was moved to higher ground. Since the relocation, the church structure has undergone many renovations, clearly a testament to the parish's faith and commitment. Log church buildings were very common in the early 1800s. Many were crudely constructed; however, this church was well built by skilled craftsmen, as evidenced by the expertly flush-cut dovetail corner joints.

It is also apparent that not long ago a new steeply pitched porch roof was added to help protect the front door area and provide a place to hang the large brass bell beneath.

CHURCHES OF ST. CECILIA
AND ST. KATERI

Tachie

For many thousands of years, Pacific salmon have returned to the mouth of the Fraser River, various species at different times during the summer and early fall. They begin the annual inland migration by ascending the mighty Fraser River and beyond to five major watersheds in the Fraser Basin.

This is also the time when First Nations communities along the Fraser tributaries prepare for the harvest of a sought-after food source essential to their sustenance.

The community of Tachie, also known as Tl'Axt'en, which essentially means people by the edge of the bay, is located along the north shore of Stewart Lake at the outflow of the Tachie River.

Tachie is a progressive and well-organized community that owns and manages an elementary school, health centre, public works department, community hall and fire hall. They also have within their community an RCMP office and two churches.

The original Church of St. Cecilia was constructed during the late 1800s in the old part of the village near the river. After many recurring flooding episodes throughout the early life of this church, it was dismantled and moved farther up the bank and reassembled. This lovely, predominantly white church with red trim stands today as a prominent landmark, facing gorgeous views of Stewart Lake.

Rarely does one encounter two functioning churches within a First Nation community, however, this one has two. St. Kateri Church is situated in a more central location in the newer area of the reserve and was probably built in the 1960s. It's painted in the same colour scheme as St. Cecilia, but is a much larger building than its counterpart. It's a little more simplified in design but equally welcoming.

OUR LADY OF THE HOLY ROSARY
- 1911

Moricetown

Moricetown, named after missionary Father Adrien G. Morice, is one of the few places in British Columbia that make it easy to visually experience the culture and traditions of a First Nation community, just by stopping at a small roadside pullout along Highway 16, 31 km northwest of Smithers. The pullout provides an impressive view that overlooks what is considered to be a gem in the wilderness, where the highway literally cuts through the middle of this heritage settlement of the Wet´suwet´en First Nation.

Besides the basic amenities one might expect, there is an RV camping facility, a cultural centre/museum and a local craft shop. However, the real treasure here is the natural beauty of the area and the historic native fishery that has been going for hundreds of years. The focal point of this very active community is the Morice Canyon, where the Bulkley River flows.

During the spring runoff, the Bulkley turns into a ragging torrent that is compressed through the narrow gorge of the canyon, spilling out to form breathtaking waterfalls.

In the fishing season, the arrival of the chinook and sockeye begins in mid-July, followed by coho and steelhead by month's end, as well as a chum salmon on occasion during August and early September. Fishing methods include basketry traps, dip-nets, harpoons and gaff hooks. Traditional outdoor fish-drying racks and smokers can be seen just below the access bridge that crosses the river.

One hundred years ago, under the leadership of their beloved priest Father Morice, the community built a new church, Our Lady of the Rosary. This rather large, century-old church has been well maintained and is architecturally characteristic of church buildings in the province.

Pointed-arch stained-glass windows dominate the façade as well as both sides of the main structure; it is a powerful attraction.

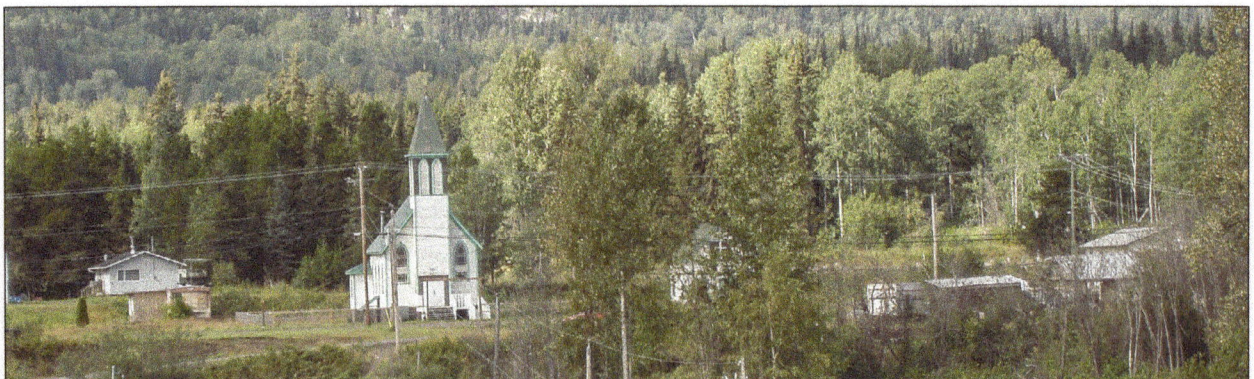

SALVATION ARMY CHURCH
- 1898

Sik-E-Dakh – Glen Vowell

Glen Vowell, originally identified on early maps of the area as Glenvowell Salvation Army Mission, was established in the late 1800s by Arthur Stewart Vowell, surveyor of the site. Glen is a Scottish word that means a narrow hidden valley, in this case one commonly known as the Kispiox Valley.

The name preferred by those who live here is Sik-E-Dakh, loosely translated as bright lights behind mountain. Due east of the village is the Babine Mountain Range and Nine Mile Mountain, and imposing, 5,000-feet-plus mass popular with hikers. Sik-E-Dakh, home to a Gitxsan community, is 12 km north of Hazelton.

More than 100 years ago, in 1898, the people of Sik-E-Dakh built a new church here with the assistance of the Salvation Army. It is a bold structure that uniquely presents itself as a proud

stronghold where people can congregate. Striking tall towers with pyramid-style rooftops bring together an appropriate and welcoming entrance to this grand building.

Once inside, one is immediately drawn to the incredible stained-wood vaulted ceiling and walls. Beautiful old hardwood pews and other distinguishing features abound in this great assembly area. It is indeed a warm and welcoming place of worship.

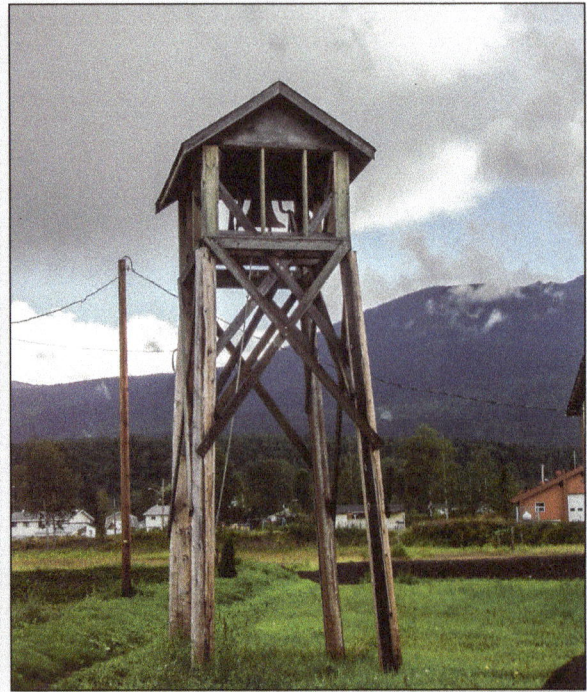

PIERCE MEMORIAL
UNITED CHURCH

Kispiox

The land of the Gitxsan First Nation people and their community is located at the juncture of the Kispiox and Skeena Rivers. From 1865 to 1867 it was also the site of Fort Stager, a Hudson's Bay Company fur trading and warehouse facility.

Fort Stager was an integral supply post for the ill-fated Collins Telegraph Line that came through the area. The plan was to link communications between Europe and America via Russia, but construction ceased at Fort Stager in 1867 when the project was supplanted by a more economical trans-Atlantic cable.

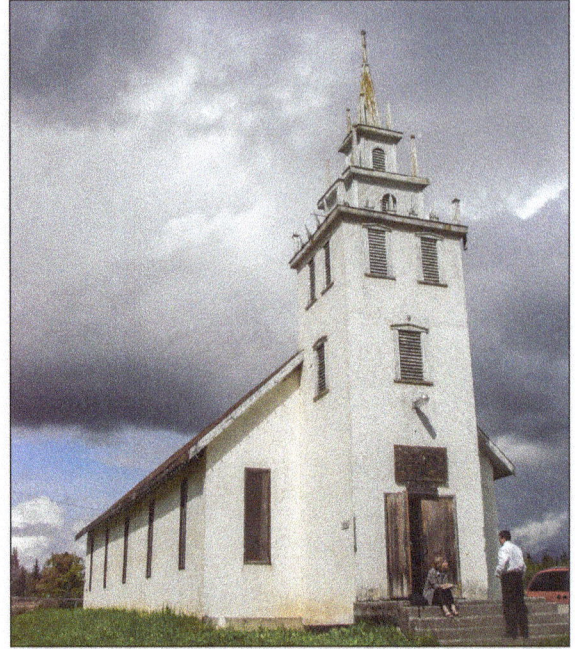

Today, a drive through the Kispiox village reveals buildings including an elementary school, fire hall, cultural centre, gas bar and a community radio station. One will also encounter a large array of old and new totem poles carved by some of the best Gitxsan master carvers.

This first-class community is also the home of Pierce Memorial United Church, which has served people in the region since 1949. Pierce Memorial replaced an earlier church by the same name that burned to the ground in 1946. The church was named after Reverend William H. Pierce.

This stately old church is an impressive-looking structure. The double entrance doors are incorporated into an imposing triple-tiered bell tower. Each tier is adorned with many pinnacles of various sizes. A short, simple spire completes the overall architectural goal.

The interior presents an appealing and harmonious setting with a hint of aboriginal embellishment.

ST. PETER'S ANGLICAN CHURCH - 1900

- Old Hazelton –

By 1900, Hazelton had become a very important transportation hub for the distribution of goods and services to inland communities to the east.

Stern-wheelers regularly plied the dangerous waters of the Skeena River from Port Essington on the coast to the jumping-off point at Hazelton.

Travellers on board these boats could see St. Peter's Church as they approached the river bank at Hazelton. Today, as in the past, this attractive landmark stands proudly overlooking the Skeena River.

This superbly built church was built under the direction of Bishop William Ridley and was opened on October 4, 1900. It remains the oldest standing building in Hazelton.

It has a three-storey-high, four-pinnacled, crenellated bell tower that dominates the front façade. The bell was shipped from Leicestershire, England, and is today very much intact.

The windows and louvered tower vents are in the gothic style, and the structure is nicely covered with flat beveled clapboard. The side entrance door is also designed in the gothic tradition and is set well into the outside wall of the tower.

The arched doors are attractively framed, complete with diagonal tongue-and-groove boards.

The roof has two short, four-sided, louvered air vents mounted on the ridge, as well as a small white cross near the gable end.

CHURCH OF
ST. MARY MAGDALENE

Hazelton

Situated at the northwest corner of the province near the confluence of the Skeena and Bulkley rivers are the Hazeltons—three separate towns named Hazelton, New Hazelton and South Hazelton.

Hazelton, also locally known as Old Hazelton, was at the head of a navigation network and a thriving transportation hub on the Skeena River during the later years of the fur trade and the burgeoning frontier years of the gold rush period. This was also the time when the ill-fated Collins Overland Telegraph Line was being constructed.

Mountain views in all directions showcase this picturesque valley, widely acknowledged as one of the most beautiful places in British Columbia.

A short distance from this historic terminus is another equally historic settlement called Hagwilget – meaning home of the quiet people. Close to this community, one can experience a walk or ride over the Hagwilget Canyon by way of an all steel, one-lane suspension bridge that spans the Bulkey River. There have been as many as three or perhaps four bridges built in this location over the years. The original bridge crossing was built by the local residents hundreds of years ago, prior to first contact. It was a vital

trading link between coastal and inland First Nations communities.

Another attraction is the reconstructed Ksan Historical Village and interpretive centre as well as a score of artfully carved totem poles, all of which bring alive the ancient traditions and culture of the Ksan people.

To the south, one can see the stunning Hagwilet Peak, which towers over the Hazeltons, a phenomenal landmass that boldly stands well over 6,000 feet and can be seen for miles around, especially from the front door of St. Mary Magdalene Church, which stands high up on a hill overlooking the reserve.

This church rises high above the landscape with its awe-inspiring, three-tier, box-like bell tower and conical spire. It has arched louvered openings in the third tier and is adorned with large pinnacles at each corner.

Adornments to the second tier include an attractive stylized sunburst with an overlaid cross, immediately above a sizable arched window. St. Mary Magdalene Church is an inspiring structure that can be seen from all areas of the community.

As with most active churches of this period, expansion becomes inevitable. St. Peter's is no exception; it too was under construction during our visit, as can been seen here.

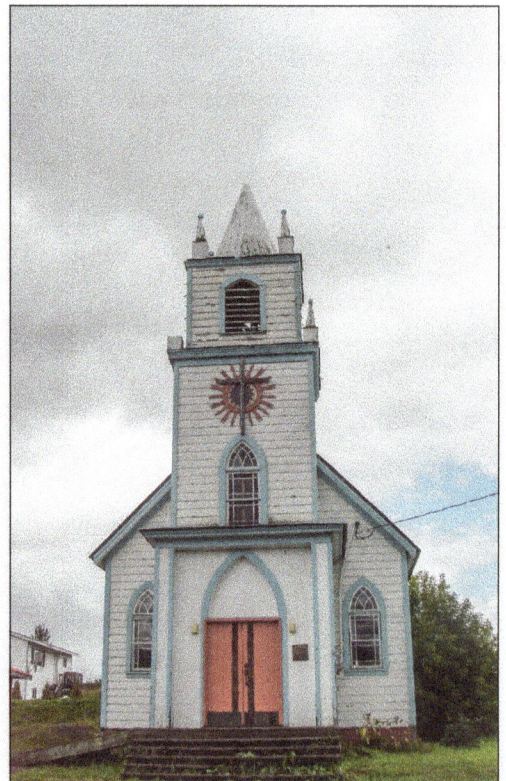

UNITED CHURCH
OF GITSEGUKLA

Skeena Crossing

Between Hazelton and the junction of the Stewart Cassiar Highway 37, is the community of Gitsegukla, sometimes referred to as Skeena Crossing. The community takes its name from the nearby Gitsegukla River, which enters the Skeena River. From first contact through to the early 1900s, this area was a hive of activity the likes of which the aboriginal villages along the Skeena had never seen before. Traders, gold-seekers and homesteaders tramped the trails and travelled by paddle-wheelers from the coast to the jumping-off point at Hazelton.

In 1911, a bridge was built by the Grand Trunk Pacific Railway as the railway made its way west to the Pacific coast, effectively supplanting paddle-wheelers. Having progressed from frontier First Nations trails to wagon roads and paved highways, getting around the province from here can now accomplished in a few hours in any direction. Certainly not like the days of the 19th and early 20th century, where weeks or months were the norm.

Along Highway 16, at the village of Gitsegukla, with its grand array of totem poles, stands Gitsegukla United Church. It was built in the late 1920s and remodeled inside and out about the mid-1970s. The façade has been substantially altered from its original design, in particular the lower section of the bell tower. It was extended outward to align with the outer walls of the main body of the building. A portico has been added, providing protection from snow and heavy rain. Flanking the main doors, small, rectangular windows have replaced the original arched windows.

The top two-thirds of the bell tower and the two smaller roof-mounted matching towers have essentially remained unaltered. Fixed to the top of the three metal-clad spires are decorative finials stylized in the shape of a candle flame. It seems apparent that, throughout the history of this fine old church, expansion and remodeling became necessary to meet the community's needs.

ST. PAUL'S CHURCH

Kitwanga

Kitwanga, also referred to as Gitwangax First Nation, is located at the junction of Highway 16 and the Stewart Cassiar Highway 37. The community there at one time had a Hudson's Bay Company fort, which later became a railway station for the Grand Trunk Pacific Railway, which came through the area in the early 1900s. The Canadian National Railway–CNR now operates in this region.

A few miles north on Highway 37 is the Gitwangak Battle Hill National Historic Site. Oral history imparts the story of a warrior chief who constructed a fort-like structure on this site 200 years ago. It had many cedar dwellings and palisade walls on top of a hill which provided a 360-degree view of the valley below, as well as an excellent vantage point to monitor the Kitwanga River.

The fortification made it possible to carry out surprise attacks on coastal peoples who used the ancient grease trail for trade and unscrupulous activities; this trail passed close by the base of Battle Hill. This fortification is without question a First Nations National Historic Site, but all that

Bell tower and church at Kitwanga, August 2007.

Bell tower and church at Kitwanga, 1962.
Photo from *Old Wooden Buildings*, Hancock House, 1978.

remains visible today is a large, grassy dome-like hill. Apparently the fort was destroyed by fire in the early 1800s. It's nevertheless a great stop of interest, complete with interpretive signs, photographs, wooden stairways and a viewing platform for visitors passing through the area.

Within the village of Kitwanga is St. Paul's Anglican Church, built in 1893 and well looked after for more than a hundred years. The building has a most interesting and remarkable design. It combines a variety of architectural elements not often seen in the region. The façade unites a covered porch entryway, four large, traditional pointed-arch windows, and a single bell tower capped with a tall, slim, four-sided bell-cast style steeple. In addition, four buttress-like elements have been incorporated into the lower outside corners of the tower, establishing a unique composition.

Of particular interest are the inverted turned finials that accent all the inside and outside corners of the main roof line, a delicate treatment for a very impressive building.

Out front of St. Paul's is a large stand-alone bell tower built by residents of the reserve, a great example of native carpentry art, very intricate in design with a multitude of angular applied wooden elements.

HOLY TRINITY CHURCH

Stoney Creek

The Stoney Creek people are of the Dakelh (Carrier) Nation, which pioneered this area long before the white man arrived. Simon Fraser made first contact and traded with the local inhabitants in 1806. The term carrier was said to have been given to the people by the fur traders to reflect a custom that when a man died, his widow would carry around his cremated bones and ashes for a year of mourning.

Just south of the town of Vanderhoof is the former Stoney Creek Band, whose preferred name today is Saik'uz First Nation. The community is exceedingly entrepreneurial and well-structured, with main activities being forestry, firefighting and construction. They also have a general store, school, community multiplex, a health centre, band office and a church.

A few miles due east of this community on Highway 16, at a place called Weneez, is a cairn bearing a brass plaque that reads: "Weneez is a Carrier Indian word meaning 'CENTRE.' It was chosen as the name for the surrounding community in honour of the original inhabitants of central B.C., the Carrier Indian Tribe." This cairn denotes the exact geographic centre of British Columbia.

The Holy Trinity Church at Stoney Creek is a large building adjacent to Stoney Creek, which flows through the centre of the community. Holy Trinity is a relatively modern structure, simple in design and quite functional to meet the needs of the people there. The façade is graced by a large, squat-looking bell tower, combined with a low-angled, peaked roof that is deeply recessed into the main building. Overall presentation is proportionately balanced and very inviting, a respectable building.

ST. PIUS X CHURCH

Shelley – Fort George

Long before the establishment of Simon Fraser's 1807 fur trading fort near the confluence of the Nechako and Fraser Rivers, the area there was the homeland of the Lheidli T'Enneh First Nation, formerly known as the Fort George Band.

Around the early part of 1912, the Grand Trunk Pacific Railway negotiated the purchase of the aboriginal village of the Fort George Reserve and its store. This arrangement literally split the new frontier town of Central Fort George, South Fort George and Fort George. The Hudson's Bay Company at Fort George closed its operations in 1915, thus ending a period of trade that had lasted more than a hundred years.

The "people from the confluence of the rivers" were relocated at a place called Shelly, about 16 miles up the Fraser River. This relocation allowed the advancement of the railway through the fledging town of Fort George, which eventually became incorporated under the name Prince George. By 1913, a beautiful Catholic church was built at Shelley, which stood out like a cathedral in the wilderness along the north bank of the Fraser River.

St. Pius X is a great example of quality workmanship of the early 1900s. The façade is brilliantly structured with a tall, square bell tower that incorporates double main doors and arched upper windows, and is capped with a very classical machine-pressed metal covering at the base of the belfry and dome. Matching treatments were applied to the front corner towers. Several years ago, the stained-glass windows were saved for posterity. The beautiful handcrafted windows were carefully crated for safe storage at the Exploration Place and

Museum in Prince George. This was a step that recognized the heritage value these precious items hold for the Lheidli T'Enneh people of Shelly. The windows and many other items of great importance were originally purchased by the Shelly community when the church was built.

Sadly, this once highly revered church has slowly withered away over many decades to a point of abandonment and decay.

ST. PATRICK'S
CATHOLIC CHURCH

Fraser Lake West – Stellako

Located at the west end of Fraser Lake are two side-by-side communities, one aboriginal and the other non-aboriginal. The Stellat'en First Nation has for centuries occupied this area of the lake and the Stellako River system. The estuary there is alive during the spring with nesting waterfowl, especially the largest of them all, the trumpeter swans. Large annual salmon runs can be seen in the Stellako River during the summer months as the fish make their way to Francois Lake to the west.

Fabulous recreational opportunities exist along the north shore of the lake, along with hiking trails and ancient lava flows. Outdoor enthusiasts can visit an extinct volcano at Red Rock, tramp the Ormond Creek Canyon Trail, and enjoy camping opportunities; all are available to the adventurous-minded rover.

Along Highway 16 near the Stellat'en community is the town of Fort Fraser, named after Simon Fraser, explorer and fur trader. It is one of the oldest settlements in British Columbia. Pioneer settlers began coming here as far back as 1806 in the lucrative fur-trade days of the Hudson's Bay Company. The town was established a short distance away from Fraser's historic post.

Over a hundred years later, the Grand Trunk Pacific Railway steamed through the Stellat'en First Nation community on its way to the coast. Today, near the railway line is a small Roman Catholic church that serves the Stellako River people.

St. Patrick's Church is a humble structure, relatively modern and possibly built in the 1950s or 1960s. The exterior stucco walls are fitted with plain, rectangular stained-glass windows throughout. The interior walls of the nave are finished in wooden paneling and completed with appropriate furniture and other adornments.

ST. PETER'S CATHOLIC CHURCH

Fraser Lake – Nadleh Whu´ten – Nautley

At the east end of Fraser Lake is the homeland of the Nadleh Whut´en First Nation and Beaumont Provincial Park, site of the historic Fort Fraser.

The Nadleh Whut´en people have been on the land in this region since time immemorial. Their fishery operated much the same as that of the Stellat'en people at the west end of the lake, where they harvested their needs from the shortest river in the world—the half-mile long Nautley River.

Northwest of the community, ancient aboriginal pictographs can be seen less than a mile away from the main village, but receiving permission to access them is essential.

Adjacent to Nadleh Whut´en is Beaumont Provincial Park and the site of Simon Fraser's historic North West Company Fort, established in 1806. In 1817, it was consumed by fire. As a result of the coalition with the NWC, the Hudson's Bay Company acquired the fort site in 1821; five years later the post was rebuilt, which also included a bastion. By 1829, Fort Fraser boasted of being the most valuable enterprise in New Caledonia. The aboriginal people of the region were the main fur traders with the NWC and subsequently the Hudson's Bay Company.

In the centre of the Nadleh Whut´en community is a large building that essentially forms the focal point of the reserve: St. Peter's Catholic Church. The church was built in 1914 at the time when the Grand Trunk Pacific Railway was under construction in this area.

The exterior appearance of this fine old church is very eye-catching. The striking white and bright blue colours dominate and accentuate the lovely architectural elements. Three distinct elements of the bell tower together present an interesting façade: a tapered front entryway; a large, square, open-louvered drum section; and a four-sided spire nicely adorned with small crosses at each corner. Round louvered openings on each side of the spire presumably enhance the sounds of the bell when rung.

Flanking the tower are arched lancet-style windows, returned eaves and basic pointed-arch windows on each side of the building. A large five-pointed star with electrified lighting is noticeably mounted over the open louvered drum; it appears to be a recently added feature.

OUR LADY OF THE PLAINS

Grassy Plains – Francois Lake

At a place called Grassy Plains, near the south bank of Francois Lake, is a beautiful open-range landscape with stunning northern views. On this land stands an attractive, bright blue, modern crafted building by the name of Our Lady of the Plains. Recent enhancements have been added to the front entrance: new stairs, hand rails and an elaborately built bell tower and spire mounted on the existing porch roof, which appears to have been built to replace the old four-posted freestanding bell tower at the left front corner of the building. Our Lady of the Plains is truly an outstanding landmark of the area.

Burns Lake is the nearest main service centre, located on Highway 16, a short 24-km ferry ride across the lake to the north shore.

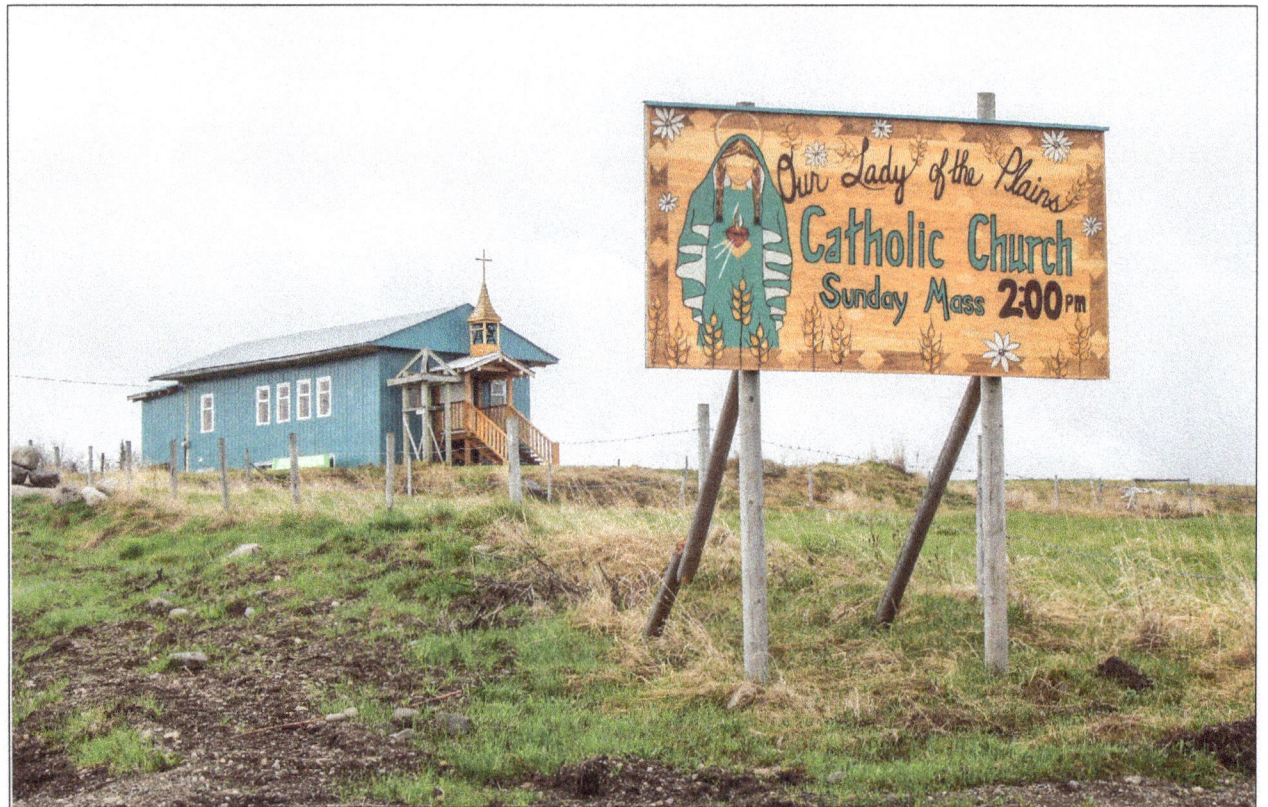

ST. AIDAN'S CHURCH

Telegraph Creek

In the late 1800s an Anglican mission known as the Upper Stikine was established at a place called Glenora. By 1899, the Hudson's Bay Company built a store there, and in 1901–1902 a second store was established at Telegraph Creek to challenge its HBC competitor downriver. A year later, the Glenora HBC store was closed, literally cut in half and moved about 12 miles (19 km) upriver by teams of horses to Telegraph Creek, a more central area for business at that time. This historic HBC post operates today as the Stikine Riversong Lodge and Café.

Telegraph Creek became the main supply center of the region, especially since the arrival of the Collins Telegraph Line, which also made this head-of-navigation point its main supply depot on the Stikine River. Paddle-wheelers brought thousands of would-be miners, speculators and supplies to this historic town during the gold rush period.

In 1921 a Mission House was built at Telegraph Creek, which was supplanted in 1924 by St. Aidan's Anglican Church. St Aidan's continues to this day to be a spiritual centre for all people there. The population at Telegraph Creek is about 300 First Nations people and about 50 non-aboriginals.

Inside St. Aidan's Church a banner hangs over the altar commemorating the 60th anniversary of St. Mary the Virgin Tahltan 1937–1997. St. Mary's is located at Old Tahltan to the east.

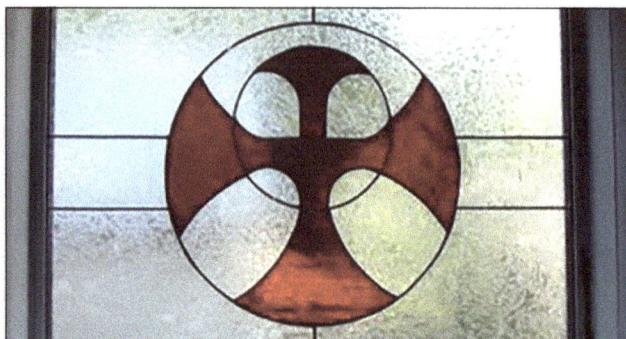

ST. MARY'S
THE VIRGIN TAHLTAN CHURCH -
1937

Old Tahltan

The road to Tahltan is rough, steep, and has countless switchbacks that will test the will of most travellers to the area. This winding road generally follows the Grand Canyon of the Stikine River, a canyon with vertical drops of nearly a thousand feet to the water below.

At the confluence of the Tahltan and Stikine Rivers, high up on the escarpment, is the old Tahltan community site and traditional lands used by the Tahltan First Nation people, whose history here extends beyond the reach of memory.

From this community one can view Mount Edziza, an ancient volcano with a landscape of old lava flows and cinder cones. This rugged, 8,000-foot, very conspicuous attraction now lies dormant. Hundreds of years ago, the mountain was a valuable source for the Tahltan of obsidian, a glass-like material from cooled molten lava. This material was shaped into cutting blades of all shapes and sizes and traded for goods from other First Nations people from the Pacific Coast.

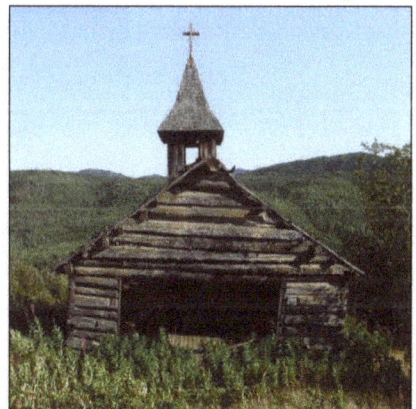

St. Mary's Church was established by 1903 and served the Old Tahltan village for 34 years, after which, for unknown reasons, it was seemingly abandoned. A second church dedicated July 13, 1937, called St. Mary the Virgin Tahltan, was built very close by and was in continuous use for 60 years. Both churches are now abandoned and in a state of disrepair. St. Aidan's Church at Telegraph Creek provides regular services to all communities of the district.

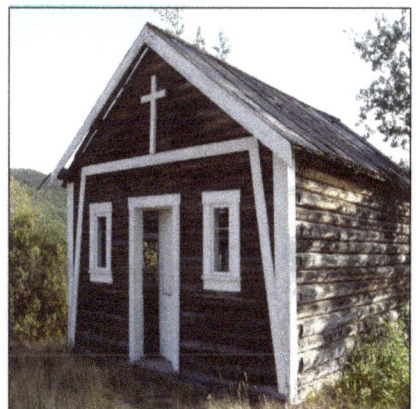

GLOSSARY

BASIC CHURCH & ARCHITECTURAL TERMINOLOGY

Basic Church Terminology

Altar - Communion table, the central fixture of worship in the church.

Apse - The area (often under a dome) that forms a semicircular or polygonal end point to the church, where the altar is placed.

Belfry - That part of a steeple, or other building, in which a bell or bells are hung.

Bell tower - A structure to house a bell.

Bench - A type of seat with no back, often used in place of a pew.

Chancel - That part of a church where the altar or communion table is placed, usually having a railing in front.

Choir - The part of a church appropriated for singers, usually between the nave and the chancel.

Church - A house consecrated to the worship of God among Christians.

Confessional - The place where a priest sits to hear confessions.

Lych gate - A roofed gateway to a churchyard, used as a resting place for a coffin before burial.

Lectern - A desk from which the Bible is read publicly.

Nave - The middle or body of a church, extending from the baluster or rail of the choir to the principal entrance.

Pew – A long bench with a back, placed in rows in a church.

Pergola – A structure consisting of posts supporting an open roof.

Sacristy – A room in a church where sacred utensils, vestments etc. are kept; now called a vestry.

Sanctuary - A place of protection; a sacred asylum or shelter. It may refer to the main meeting place of a church, or more specifically the part where the altar is placed, encompassed by a balustrade.

Shrine – A place regarded as holy or a container holding sacred objects. A tomb, altar or a statue may be placed in a shrine for worshippers to reflect upon.

Stations of the Cross - A pictorial representation of a series of 14 images in the story of the Crucifixion of Jesus, to help worshippers focus their devotion.

Vestry - A room or office in which the vestments and sacred utensils are kept, and where meetings are held.

Basic Architecture Terminology

Arch - A portion of the circumference of a circle or other curve; a concave or hollow structure of a window or doorway.

Balustrade - A row of balusters (short pillars or columns) joined by a rail, serving as a fence or enclosure for altars, balconies, staircases, terraces, and tops of buildings.

Bell roof - A roof shaped like a bell, also known as a bell-cast roof.

Beam - The largest or a principal piece of timber in a building which lies across the walls and supports the main rafters.

Board - A piece of timber sawed thin, and of considerable length and breadth.

Batten - A piece of wood from one inch to seven inches broad, and from half an inch to two inches and a half thick.

Bracket - A right-angled support attached to and projecting from a wall for holding a shelf, lamp, or other object; may be wood, steel or stone.

Bull's-eye window - A small circular window or opening. A thick, round piece of glass segmented into multiple wedges, each piece tapering from a wide arch down to a point at the opposite end, culminating at a small round piece referred to as an eye.

Buttress - A projecting support of stone or brick built against a wall on the outside.

Canopy – An ornamental covering hanging above an altar.

Cantilever - A long bracket or beam framed into the front of side of the church and projecting from it to support a balcony, cornice, moulding or eaves.

Capital - The uppermost decorative part of a column, pillar or pilaster.

Casement - A portion of a window-sash made to open or turn on hinges.

Cladding - An exterior covering of a wall.

Clapboard - A thin board ready-cut for covering buildings.

Column - A long, round pillar of wood or stone used to support or adorn a building, composed of a base, a shaft and a capital.

Cornice - An ornamental molding around the wall of a room just below the ceiling.

Cresting - A decorative element, often of metal or wood, located at the peak of a roof.

Crocket – A series of repetitive ornamental designs, often imitating curved or bent foliage, placed at the angle of gables, pinnacles, canopies, etc.

Cruciform – Form of a cross.

Cupola – A spherical vault on the top of a dome or roof.

Dentil – A decorative series of small, rectangular blocks resembling teeth, used under the soffit of a cornice.

Dormer - A window pierced through a sloping roof, the frame being placed vertically on the rafters.

Dovetail - A manner of fastening boards and timbers together by letting one piece fit into another in the form of a dove's tail, or reversed wedge.

Drum – A circular or polygonal wall supporting a dome or cupola; may be louvred to allow the sound of a bell to emanate.

Eaves - The edge or lower border of a roof that overhangs the wall and casts off the water that falls on the roof.

Façade – The front or face of a building.

Fanlight – A semicircular window with glazing bars radiating out like an open fan, usually located over a door.

Fascia - A board or sheet metal band that is placed under the roof edge in a vertical position.

Finial - The decorative crowning point of a pinnacle or spire in gothic architecture; often with elements that resemble foliage.

Frame - The timbers fitted and joined for the purpose of supporting the roof.

Fretwork - An interlaced decorative design carved from wood with a fret saw or similar device.

Gable - The triangular end of a roof, from the eaves to the top.

Lancet - A high and narrow window, pointed at the top.

Lattice - A structure of crossed wooden or metal strips arranged to form a diagonal pattern of open spaces between the strips.

Lintel – A horizontal piece that spans the opening between two vertical supports, such as the top part of a door frame.

Louvre - An opening crossed by bars of wood to exclude rain but allow the passage of sound from the bells.

Lozenge – Rhombus or diamond shape, found in mouldings.

Moulding - Ornamental element that defines or outlines the edges and surfaces on a projecting or receding part of the building design, such as a cornice.

Mullion - A slender piece of material that divides window panes.

Niche - A cavity, hollow, or recess within the thickness of a wall, designed to hold a statue or other ornament.

Ogee - A moulding consisting of a round and a hollow, like a wave.

Palladian window - A three-part window with a tall rounded-arch center window flanked by smaller rectangular windows.

Parapet – A low wall along the roof of a building.

Pediment – A triangular or semicircular ornament that forms a finishing gable at the front of a building or a decoration over gates, windows and niches.

Pilaster - A square column, usually set within a wall and projecting only a fourth or fifth of its width.

Pinnacle – A small spire.

Portal - The framework or arch of a door or gate, an opening for entrance.

Portico - A covered space enclosed or supported by columns at the entrance of a building.

Post - A piece of timber set upright, usually larger than a stake and extended to support something else.

Post and beam - A system of vertical and horizontal posts and beams, of which spaces in between are filled in with other kinds of material.

Rafter - A roof timber that extends from the plate or top of a wall toward the ridge and serves to support the covering of the roof.

Returned eave - An eave that continues at a right angle across an adjacent wall surface.

Rose window - A large circular stained-glass window with glass elements radiating from the centre.

Sash - The frame or main structure of a window into which the panes of glass are set.

Scissor truss - A truss formed in a scissor-like fashion to support a high-pitched roof, allowing for a high ceiling.

Shed-roof - A roof formed by rafters sloping between a high and a low wall.

Soffit - The underside of a lintel or eave, or the horizontal surface of an arch between columns.

Spire – A tapering conical or pyramidal structure on the top of the church.

Steeple – A tall tapering structure topped by a spire, often incorporating a belfry and other components.

Studs – Vertical timbers in a building's wall, inserted between posts to support the beams.

Tie bar - A piece of timber or metal rod for binding two bodies or structures together; sometimes steel cable is used.

Transom window - A window having a horizontal mullion or cross-bar in it.

Vault - A continued arch, or an arched roof. Vaults are of various kinds: circular, elliptical, single, double, cross and diagonal.

Veranda - A kind of open portico, formed by extending a sloping roof beyond the main building.

Wainscotting - The lining of wooden boards on walls, usually on the lower third of the wall.

INDEX

REGION – FIVE:			PAGE
CARIBOO CHILCOTIN COAST			
St. Kateri Tekakwitha – 1984	Roman Catholic	Alexandria - West Bank	163
St. Paul's Church – 1907	Roman Catholic	Alexandria - East Bank	165
Church of the Immaculate Conception – 1950s	Roman Catholic	Dog Creek	169
St. Theresa's of the Child Jesus –1880s	Roman Catholic	Alkali Lake	171
St. Augustine's Church – 1991	Roman Catholic	Canim Lake	173
Our Lady of Good Counsel	Roman Catholic	Soda Creek - Williams Lake	175
Church of the Immaculate Conception – 1895	Roman Catholic	Sugar Cane - Williams Lake	177
St. John the Baptist – 1904	Roman Catholic	Stone - Hanceville	179
Sacred Heart of Jesus	Roman Catholic	Anaham - Alexis Creek	181
Visitation of the Blessed Virgin Mary Church	Roman Catholic	Anahim Lake	185
Catholic Church - 1892	Roman Catholic	Nazko	187
St. Thomas the Apostle Church	Roman Catholic	Toosey - Risky Creek	189
St. Peter's Church	Roman Catholic	Red Bluff - Quesnel	191

REGION – SIX:			PAGE
NORTHERN			
Our Lady of Good Hope – 1873	Roman Catholic	Necoslie - Fort St. James	197
Holy Cross Church	Roman Catholic	Binche	201
Churches of St. Cecilia and St. Kateri	Roman Catholic	Tachi	203
Our Lady of the Holy Rosary – 1911	Roman Catholic	Moricetown	205
Salvation Army Church – 1898	Salvation Army	Sik-E-Dakh - Glen Vowell	207
Pierce Memorial United Church	United Church	Kispiox	209
St. Peter's Anglican Church – 1900	Anglican	Old Hazelton	211
Church of St. Mary Magdalene	Roman Catholic	Hagwilget - Hazelton	213
United Church of Gitsegukla	United Church	Gitsegukla - Hwy 16 West	215
St. Paul's Church	Anglican	Kitwanga	217
Holy Trinity Church	Roman Catholic	Stoney Creek - Vanderhoof	221
St. Pius X Church	Roman Catholic	Shelley - Fort George	223
St. Patrick's Catholic Church	Roman Catholic	Stellako - Fraser Lake	225
St. Peter's Catholic Church	Roman Catholic	Nautely - Fraser Lake	227
Our Lady of the Plains	Roman Catholic	Grassy Plains - Francois Lake	229
St. Aidan's Church	Anglican	Old Tahltan	231
St. Mary's The Virgin Tahltan Church - 1937	Anglican	Telrgraph Creek	233

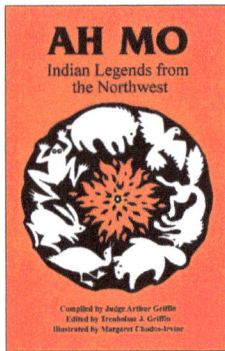

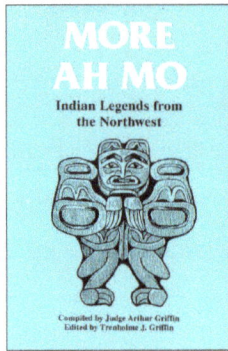

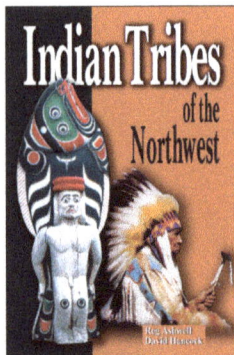

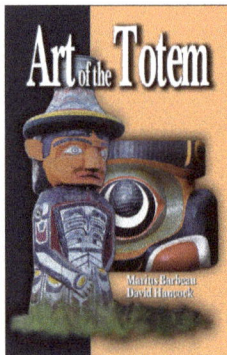

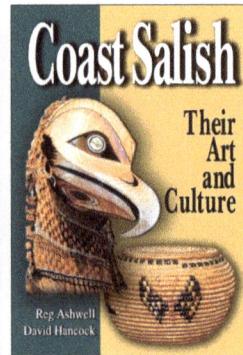

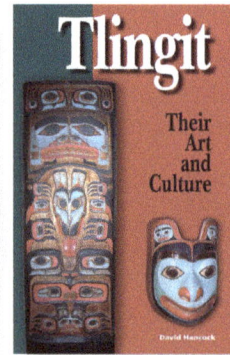

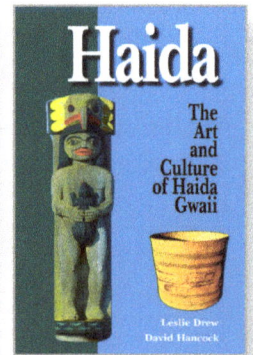

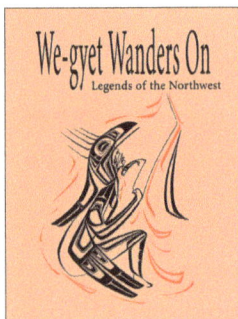

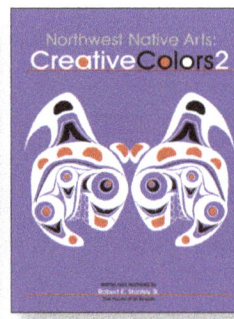

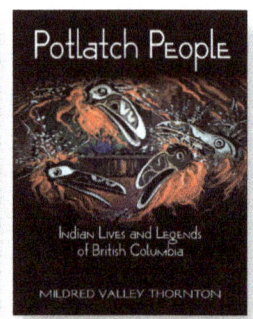